Children with Communication Disorders

Revised Edition

Prathibha Karanth

With a Foreword by
M. N. Hegde

Orient BlackSwan

Children with Communication Disorders

ORIENT BLACKSWAN PRIVATE LIMITED

Registered Office
3-6-752 Himayatnagar, Hyderabad 500 029 (A.P.), INDIA
E-mail: centraloffice@orientblackswan.com

Other Offices
Bangalore, Bhopal, Bhubaneshwar, Chandigarh, Chennai, Ernakulam, Guwahati,Hyderabad, Jaipur, Kolkata, Lucknow, Mumbai, New Delhi, Noida, Patna

First published 2009
This Revised Edition 2010
Reprinted 2011
ISBN 978 81 250 3866 5

Typeset in 12/15 pt. New Century Schoolbook

Typeset by
InoSoft Systems
NOIDA

Printed in India at
Rakmo Press (P) Ltd.
New Delhi

Published by
Orient Blackswan Private Limited
1/24 Asaf Ali Road
New Delhi 110 002
E-mail: delhi@orientblackswan.com

Dedicated to
Kota Shivarama Karanth
For the inspiration that he was

Contents

Foreword

The speech and hearing profession in India began in the 1960s, and it is now well established. Nonetheless, clinical facilities pertaining to speech and hearing are limited to large cities. In many parts of the country, the common people as well as related professionals are not familiar with clinical services offered to remediate speech, language, and hearing problems in children and adults. This problem is further intensified by a lack of resources that disseminate useful information on communication disorders to various professionals and families that have a member with a communication disability. There is thus a great need of books that inform and educate professionals and consumers about disorders of communication. Therefore, I am pleased to take note of Dr Prathibha Karanth's book, which eminently fulfils this urgent need.

Although disorders of communication are found in all age groups, it is critical to understand and treat them in children. Communication disorders in children can pose significant hurdles to their social and academic success. For children with communication disorders, social interactions are not as rewarding as they are to those who speak normally. Children who cannot articulate their speech sounds, fail to learn their native language, speak with impaired fluency (stuttering), or have a voice problem may experience negative reactions from some people. Although communication disorders can be found in otherwise quite capable children, a disorder may nonetheless make children feel they are not as competent as other children. Such children may also begin to experience negative ideas and feelings about themselves, resulting in a sense of low self-esteem.

It is well known that untreated communication disorders in children, especially language disabilities, will impede academic success. Children with limited language skills tend to have difficulty learning to read and write, and therefore, fall behind their peers as they try to move through the early grades in elementary schools. Lacking a good literacy foundation, children with communication disorders are likely to progressively fall behind other children in higher grades. Furthermore, poor academic performance will, at a later point in time, limit their occupational choices. Consequently, an untreated communication disorder may lead to a life-long disability.

Communication disorders are most effectively treated in children. Early intervention is more effective than treatment offered later in life. Successful treatment will also ensure that the child will have greater success in social and academic contexts that in turn increasing the likelihood of him growing into a more confident and successful adult. Therefore, it is critical that professionals as well as family members recognise a communication disorder in a child as early as possible, and recommend early treatment for the child and support for the family. An impediment to this early intervention is a lack of knowledge or awareness of communication problems at all levels of society, as well as a lack of familiarity with speech and hearing professionals and what they can do to help.

Speech-language pathologists are the specialists who assess and treat disorders of communication. However, a child with such a disorder and his or her family may initially come in contact with other professionals. For example, pediatricians; child psychologists; preschool and elementary school teachers; special educators; developmental neurologists; child mental health professionals; and ear, nose, and throat specialists may see a child with a speech or language problem who is not yet seen by a speech-language pathologist. It would be greatly helpful if these other professionals recognise the child's problem early and counsel the family to promptly seek help from a speech-language pathologist. Dr Karanth's book will be a valuable resource to these professionals who wish to help children and families with communication disorders.

The book is an equally valuable resource to parents of children with communication disorders. Many parents may not have a clear understanding of the various disorders of communication and treatment possibilities. They may be unaware of the excellent work speech-language pathologists do in their own communities to correct speech and language problems. An introductory book on communication disorders, written in clear and simple terms, widely made available to professionals and parents alike, will help children with speech and language disorders and their families seek help as early as possible. Dr Karanth wrote this book to achieve such a worthy goal.

I cannot think of another, more capable person who could write a book like this one. Dr Karanth is a leading speech-language pathologist in India. Her research, clinical service, lucid writings, and commitment to improving the quality of life for children with communication disorders and their families is known throughout India and abroad. She has expertise in communication disorders that affect both children and adults. She has been a mentor for many young speech-language pathologists in India as she has worked as, and continues to work as, a professor in various institutes. She is a founder of an unique institute in Bangalore for children with autism. Her scientifically based program to teach communication skills to children with autism is now widely recognised as one of the most successful anywhere.

Dr Karanth's book covers a wide range of communication disorders in children, including those which are closely related to learning disabilities. In clear, simple, and scientifically accurate terms, she describes not only speech and language disorders, but also hearing impairment, intellectual disabilities (mental retardation), cerebral palsy, autism spectrum disorders, and neuropsychiatric problems that are associated with speech and language problems. Dr Karanth's book offers useful and current information for both parents and other professionals who might refer a child to a speech-language pathologist.

Students training to be speech-language pathologists will find this book a good introduction and overview of the discipline of speech-language pathology. Instructors in various academic programs in speech and hearing may find this as a valuable resource for students and recommend this for their study.

It is a challenging task to simultaneously address the multiple goals this book seeks to achieve: writing for different professionals, parents, speech-language pathologists, and students in the discipline. But I am very pleased to note that in writing this book, Dr Karanth has met her goals admirably. Practical in its size, easy in its style, and comprehensive in its coverage, the book will interest both professionals and parents alike. Anyone who reads this book will be in a much better position to seek timely help for children with communication disorders.

M. N. Hegde

Preface

Communication skills are more important now than ever before in the history of mankind. In modern society, there is enormous social pressure on honing communication skills at all stages of life. Children who are in the process of acquiring communication skills are the most vulnerable to this social pressure. Not surprisingly, communication disorders in children are also on the rise. Also, awareness of the nature of these communication disorders, their identification and management is relatively poor in countries like India.

This book provides a simple, lucid and scientific account of the types of communication disorders that may be seen in children. It is addressed to an audience of parents, teachers and other concerned professionals such as paediatricians, ENT specialists, developmental neurologists, psychologists and special educators. It introduces the reader to the range of communication disorders that may be seen in children so as to be able to recognise them, implement preventive and remedial steps where feasible, and seek appropriate professional help where needed. It will help families and professionals to identify and support children with communication disorders across a range of settings including homes, schools and clinics. The book can also serve as an introductory text to students of the subject.

Prathibha Karanth

1

Introduction

Communication is at the core of modern society. The ability to express ourselves, our thoughts, feelings, needs, and desires and the quick and precise exchange of information between us, is the essence of communication and is critical for our survival. The many and multifaceted changes that have occurred in the means of communication, stand out as among the most important revolutions of the twentieth century, one that has had enormous and widespread impact. Success in today's society is increasingly linked to the speed and precision of communication, through a variety of mediums. Paradoxically while the importance of rapid and clear communication has increased, the awareness and understanding of the consequences of difficulties in communication has not kept pace.

Communication skills are acquired by the child in a gradual process that extends from early childhood through adulthood. Many of the core communication skills of speech and language are mastered in early childhood. Literacy and mastery over the more complex and increasingly varied communication skills follow and are dependent on exposure, training and demand. During this prolonged phase of mastery, several factors, from the biological to the environmental can interfere with the acquisition of these crucial skills.

The term 'communication disorders' encompasses a wide variety of problems in hearing, speech and language. Individuals with these disorders are unable to understand and/or use the language of their society appropriately. Communication disorders are grouped into two main categories: those with hearing disorders and those with speech-language disorders, though they need not be mutually exclusive. Hearing impairments range from a minimal loss in one ear which might interfere in hearing faint sounds to severe impairment in both ears resulting in hearing speech in a distorted way, if at all; to profound deafness. The effect of hearing impairment on speech and language varies depending both on the severity and the age at which hearing became impaired. Speech and language disorders affect the way people talk. These disorders may range from simple sound substitutions or unwanted repetitions to the complete absence of the ability to use speech and language for communication.

The overall estimate for communication disorders in school-aged children is widely agreed to be 5 to 10 per cent. This includes children with articulation disorders, voice disorders, stuttering and those with relatively minor and isolated hearing, speech and language disorders but excludes children with more severe impairments such as deafness, cerebral palsy, mental retardation and autism. Children belonging to the latter group have more severe communication disorders that are secondary to the primary impairment and are often enrolled in special schools.

The incidence of communication disorders in the population at large, including adults is estimated at 10 per cent or one out of every ten people in countries like the United States. There are no clear cut figures available for India. In India, interest in and documentation of the different types of disabilities and disorders is very recent. The earlier disability census for speech and hearing disordered considered primarily the hearing impaired with speech disorders. Not only was the range of communication disorders not considered, even developmental language disorders such as language learning disabilities were not included. Nor have the learning disabilities been included. Existing figures are therefore most likely to be gross underestimations.

Communication disorders can be characterised as delays versus disorders. A child's communication is considered delayed when the child is noticeably behind his or her peers in the acquisition of speech and/or language skills. These delays are generally comprehensive delays affecting all aspects of language and the child appears to communicate like a child younger than his age. A child with a delay in speech - language acquisition may present a variety of characteristics including the inability to follow directions, slow and unintelligent speech, and pronounced difficulties in having and sustaining a conversation.

Sometimes particular aspects of communication are affected. For instance specific aspects of communication, such as correct production of speech sounds as in a child with misarticulations, or a difficulty in maintaining fluent speech as in a child with stammering, may be affected. Communication may also be affected because of hoarseness or harshness in the speaker's voice. A child may have greater receptive (understanding) than expressive (speaking) language skills with the delay in his expressive language affecting his peer interactions. Another may have adequate mastery over the speech sounds and the grammar of the language but have difficulty in using his linguistic skills appropriately across a variety of social situations. In other instances more than one aspect of a child's communication skills may be affected. Such a child may have difficulty in following directions or instructions, pronouncing words clearly and making his intention known or expressing himself clearly and generally having difficulty in conversational exchanges, in addition to difficulties in reading and writing and remembering what was said or learnt.

Communication disorders can develop at any age. It is a common belief that children will 'outgrow' these disorders. While it is true that some children make up for the delay in onset of communication skills, not all do. It is also now documented that if communication disorders are not identified and treated early, they can become more severe. With our tendency to enrol children into preschool at increasingly younger ages, untreated problems interfere with their ability to interact with peers, affecting the child adversely and often leading to behavioural repercussions. Children with communication disorders have difficulties exchanging information with others, including their peers and teachers leading to eventual difficulties in classroom interaction and learning.

Many communication disorders result from other conditions such as hearing impairment, cerebral palsy, mental retardation, or a cleft lip and palate. Several speech and language disorders are related to these identifiable defects that the child is born with. Some are consequent to injuries and ailments acquired after birth such as head injuries, strokes, viral diseases, or the prolonged use of certain drugs. Children who are developing normally may have their communication skills arrested consequent to head injuries and trauma or due to other illnesses such as meningitis, or even as a consequence of prolonged usage of life saving drugs prescribed for other life threatening diseases such as tuberculosis. Still others such as the dysarthrias may be due to specific deficits in the controlled movements of the speech organs such as the lips, tongue and mouth.

A communication disorder in a child need not necessarily be due to a congenital or biological factor alone. Disorders like developmental language disorders and learning disabilities while suspected to be genetic or biological in origin present no clear-cut physical signs of damage. Communication disorders may also occur in the absence of an organic or biological cause. Voice disorders for instance, are often the result of improper use of the voice as in excessive screaming and yelling. Such vocal abuse if continued over a prolonged period of time could in fact end up causing organic changes such as inflammation of the vocal cords, or the formation of small growths known as nodules and polyps on the vocal cords.

Poor or inadequate speech and language models in the home environment may also result in a communication disorder. Environmental factors such as lack of stimulation and adequate exposure to language may result in a delay in speech-language acquisition. Even more important, in countries like India, are the multitude of languages that a young child is exposed to and expected to learn in childhood. While bi/multilingualism in itself seldom causes long lasting deficits in language acquisition, frequent and multiple changes in the child's early language environment can indeed result in a delay in onset of language. Frequently, however, the cause of a communication disorder in a given child is unknown.

While the more severe communication disorders such as those consequent to mental retardation or deafness in children are relatively easily recognised in early childhood, the more subtle language disorders like developmental dyslexia and pragmatic deficits are often not recognised even as the child struggles through school. Most of us are familiar with children who are born with a biological deficit such as a hearing impairment or deafness, mental retardation or cerebral palsy and are aware that they do not develop like their normal peers and that a delay in speech-language acquisition is a common concomitant of these congenital defects. However, in the recent past an increasing number of young children are being identified with difficulties in the acquisition of communication skills, not caused by any of these better known factors and are referred to as developmental language disorders (DLD). The latter are not easily identifiable.

The term developmental language disorder refers to a variety of disturbances in early language acquisition and may or may not be associated with other types of developmental disabilities. Disorders such as specific language impairment (SLI), as the term implies, refers to children in whom all else being normal, there is a specific delay in the acquisition and mastery of language in particular. Developmental disabilities such as pervasive developmental disorders (PDD) on the other hand imply a host of other difficulties including sensory-motor, behavioural and social deficits along with the communication disorder. With the advances in genetics, several other specific childhood syndromes such as fragile X, which manifest both in communication and other kinds of developmental disabilities, are now being increasingly identified and studied.

Communication disorders in children are classified into different types. Traditionally the speech-language disorders were identified with the causative factor, within the medical model, as for instance in the descriptive term 'cleft palate speech' used to refer to speech problems that are associated with a cleft palate. Others have described them as the organic versus functional, once again depending on whether a clear organic or biological factor can be associated with the speech disturbance or not. Given the broad range of causative factors, speech-language pathologists or therapists have in the past, classified these disorders as the organic versus functional.

Another common dichotomy is that of Speech versus Language disorders. Speech disorders are those in which the correct production of speech sounds are affected rendering the speech unintelligible as well as those which affect the quality of the voice and the smooth flow of speech. Language disorders are those which affect the ability to understand instructions, directions, and stories as well as to string words together to make sentences, to participate in conversations, to read and to write.

The current classification of speech-language disorders identifies four broad areas: articulation, voice, fluency and language depending on the aspect of verbal communication that is disturbed. Accordingly we have articulation disorders, fluency disorders, voice disorders and language disorders. Articulation disorders are those disorders in which the child produces incorrect sounds in a word, or omits one or more of the sounds in a word, or produces them in such a manner that the listener fails to recognise them. Articulation disorders are most commonly seen in preschool or primary school children. Fluency disorders occur when the normal smooth flow of speech is disrupted and the speaker frequently hesitates, pauses or repeats speech sounds or words. These disorders can be seen in young children in the early school years and may continue to persist into adulthood. When the volume of speech is too high or low or when there is an unpleasant hoarse/harsh or nasal quality to the voice, then a voice disorder is said to be present. Finally there are language disorders, which are characterised by a variety of deficits ranging from an overall delay in acquisition or specific difficulty developing adequate vocabulary and grammar, following instructions, difficulties in reading and expressing their ideas in speech and/or writing.

Within the four broad areas of disorders (articulation, fluency, voice and language), there are additional subtypes. At any given time, a particular child may have a number of inter-related communication disorders. For instance a child with a language disorder may have a difficulty specific to reading alone. In contrast a child with cerebral palsy may have multiple communication disorders including articulation, voice, fluency and language disorders. Many learning difficulties are now being seen as being related to specific language delays. These children often struggle with the complexities of higher order language used in academia and are at risk of academic failure

During the last century, with the increasing awareness of the pivotal role of good communication in human development, there emerged the disciplines of speech-language pathology or speech-language therapy and audiology, to cater to the needs of the many children and adults who suffered from a variety of communication disorders. The speech-language pathologist/therapist (SLP/SLT) is trained in the study of human communication and is specialised in the identification, evaluation, diagnosis and remediation of speech and language disorders in children and adults. The clinical methods used by the SLP, are dependent on the nature and severity of the problem as well as the age of the client. The audiologist is trained in the complementary skills of hearing and its assessment, as well as in the selection and fitting of suitable amplification devices such as hearing aids. SLPs and audiologists or speech and hearing specialists work in close collaboration with medical professionals such as ENT surgeons, paediatricians and neurologists as well as with educators, both special and regular, and with parents and families. They often work in hospital and clinical settings and at times in educational institutions.

Though in existence in India for over four decades, the disciplines of speech-language pathology and audiology are hardly known to the public at large and clinical services have remained inaccessible for all but a few urbanites in the metropolitan societies. When available these services are generally located in clinical setups such as hospitals. Yet a sizeable proportion of the service seekers for these clinicians come from the school going populations and it is in recognition of this fact that several hundred speech-language therapists are employed in regular schools in countries of North America and Europe. The slow, long drawn out nature of speech therapy requiring prolonged interaction between therapist and client is an additional constraint, which has led to the provision of these services within the school set up. In India, given the small number of graduates trained every year, despite the sudden increase in the number of training centres, the recruitment of speech therapists in schools does not appear to be a feasible prospect, in all but the most elitist schools; in the foreseeable future. It is therefore important that the teacher is able to understand the importance of communication disorders in school going children, identify them and refer them when needed, to appropriate specialists, as well as provide the necessary support for the child in the classroom and school environment.

In the latter half of the twentieth century, for the first time scientists from divergent disciplines such as psychology and linguistics pooled their skills in studying human language and jointly applied them to the process of language acquisition by the human child. What has emerged is a wealth of information that has highlighted what a complex and lengthy process language acquisition is. This new knowledge has had an impact on the assessment and management of communication disorders too. With the emergence of psycholinguistics, assessment procedures and tools were designed anew to tease out aspects of language acquisition in children across a wide age range from infancy to adulthood, enabling us to not only identify but also quantify the language deficit in a given child as compared to his or her peer group. This endeavour in turn led to an increasing awareness that the acquisition and mastery of language in the human being was not restricted strictly to early childhood, as was hitherto thought, but that it was a process that spread across the lifespan with emphasis on different aspects at different stages. Consequently we now have language tests that can be used for the two-year old to the ninety-year old.

This sensitivity to the lifelong changes that accrue in the use of our communication skills has led to an even greater understanding of the snowballing effects of a childhood communication disorder. No longer is a delay in speech-language acquisition seen as a temporary phenomenon that the child will 'outgrow'. Instead it is becoming increasingly clear that unless the child with a developmental lag is provided with immediate and adequate assistance, the 'lag' is likely to lead to a cascading effect, affecting not only his or her communication skills but also a range of other skills that are learnt during these crucial years, eventually affecting the quality of life of the concerned individual.

The ability to communicate is considered to be the most important characteristic that separates us from the rest of the animal kingdom and that makes us 'human'. When a child or adult has difficulty in communicating, it not only cuts them off from human society but also affects the individual in myriad ways. In a child it not only isolates him socially but also affects his cognitive/educational progress. In an adult there is both the emotional isolation and the negative effects on career prospects.

Communication disorders in children can have wide ranging educational implications. Communication skills and academic achievement are closely linked. The ability to communicate with others is critical to a young child's development and it is a prerequisite to academic learning. Some children have disorders that interfere with various aspects of their abilities to communicate. While some 'immature' speech and language patterns are a part of a child's normal development, if the child does not outgrow these problems they can interfere considerably in the child's overall academic progress. Developmental delays can and do affect acquisition of speech, language and related skills. Since language experiences are at the core of a child's mental development a developmental delay in language can have much wider impact. Communication is central to and facilitates learning. In order to absorb information a child has to be able to participate actively in communication with his peers and adults around him. Further, the acquisition of reading and writing are often based on the spoken form of speech and reciprocally contribute to the mastery of language, both of which are crucial in the building of an individual's knowledge base, not only during childhood but also extending in to adult life.

Poor academic performance in otherwise typically growing children could be the consequence of or coexist with subtle communication disorders that interfere with learning in noisy crowded classrooms. The difficulties of these children in learning to listen, speak, read and write in the classroom can result from undetected problems in language development. In addition to resulting in poor communication skills, these problems often lead to difficulties in using language for learning, thinking and planning. Timely intervention becomes a must to prevent the cascading effects of these difficulties in the child's overall development that could eventually lead to school avoidance and failure.

Intervention and therapeutic support can ameliorate these difficulties and help the children become effective communicators. Good communication skills in turn can lead to better social and academic skills and to long term effects in the lives of these children.

An intervention programme for a child with a communication disorder is generally preceded by extensive evaluations to identify the source of the communication difficulties. The assessment and management of communication disorders in children requires the cooperation of several specialists apart from the speech and hearing specialist. Among the medical personnel, paediatricians, ENT surgeons, neurologists, and child psychiatrists are those that are often required to be consulted. Where necessary and feasible this is followed by medical intervention through appropriate referrals. For several communication disorders medical intervention is not an option. The SLP then provides intervention directly. In addition SLPs also work closely with psychologists, special educators and classroom teachers in the assessment and management procedures.

Given that it is the parent and schoolteacher with whom the child spends the better part of his life during the formative years it is important that they are aware of the range of disorders that can affect a child's communication skills. Identification of a possible disorder or delay should lead to a closer look and subsequent referrals to concerned specialists, if need be. Awareness and understanding of different types of communication disorders will enable the teacher to prevent some and reduce exacerbation of others. The teacher's role however does not end there, for in the event of a communication disorder being present, the eventual outcome in terms of successful remediation will also depend on how well the teacher assists the child in generalising and stabilising the gains he has made with intervention, across his everyday life.

Speech-language therapy is directed at improving the communication skills of the individual to the extent possible. There are no 'cures' for many communication problems. However children are taught and learn to use new effective strategies to ameliorate and overcome their difficulties. The treatment procedures for communication disorders are varied and specific to the type of problem faced by a given child at a given moment. It could vary from the correction of a single speech sound to providing a nonverbal means of communication and training the child in its use if the physical conditions of the child make verbal speech impossible or extremely difficult. Electronic communication devices can be provided to nonverbal children to enable them to participate in academic and social lives despite their disability.

Children with communication disorders have been traditionally provided with support in terms of speech-language therapy in one on one individual sessions twice or thrice a week, in clinical settings. While this continues to be the case in India, in Western countries there has been an increasing tendency to provide speech-language therapy for school children within the school setting, at least for those who have relatively minor problems and for those who have been mainstreamed inspite of more severe difficulties.

This is not surprising since much of a child's day is spent at school and many of his language experiences are also likely to take place at school. The speech corrections carried out by the therapist need to be blended into the classroom and the child's overall environment. Speech language therapy is likely to be most successful when carried out in consultation and close collaboration with the child's teacher and parent. The gains made in therapy can then be carried over to the classroom and home.

If this is true of the average child with a communication disorder, the teacher has to play an even more important role in the life of the special child with a communication disorder, integrated within the regular classroom. As our society has become aware of the needs and rights of the special child, more and more of them are rightfully seeking admission into regular schools and the law upholds this right of the special child to be among his peers. The current trend is therefore toward including the child with special needs in the mainstream to the extent possible. With technological advances, students whose physical problems are so severe that they interfere with or completely inhibit communication can be trained in the use of alternate and augmentative communication devices that allow the individual to make his or her needs and wants known. Where the target of normal communication skills is not feasible, SLPs can suggest strategies and goals that are more suited for that individual's daily life and the eventual transition from school to the work place and adult life.

Regretfully, teachers in regular classrooms in India are seldom equipped to meet the needs of the special child in their classroom. Since it is our belief that it is the classroom teacher who can 'make or break' a special child's integration in to the classroom, it is important that we sensitise them to the conditions that make these children 'special' and their 'special' needs. Inclusion of children with special needs in regular classrooms should not be viewed as either charity or a mere moral obligation. The long-term consequences of mainstreaming special children to the extent possible are both social and economic in nature. There is today a shift towards intensive early intervention for children with developmental disabilities because of the documented long-term gains that they result in. These gains can be made into lasting gains only when teachers understand and further support these children during the long school years.

It is with these goals in mind that this introductory book has been compiled. We hope that it will help all concerned—professionals, teachers and parents to better understand children with communication disorders and serve the needs of both the marginally delayed/disordered and those requiring more extensive support, within the regular school set up. This chapter has introduced the reader to the major aspects of the acquisition of communication skills in children and the communication disorders that have been identified and documented in children, over the latter half of the last century. What follows in the first half of the book is a description of the relatively minor communication disorders seen in children. The latter half of the book will deal with children who have more comprehensive difficulties and require considerable amount of intervention prior to school admission with extended support during their school years.

The book has been organised into three sections. The three chapters in the first section will define and describe three commonly found speech disorders in children: articulation, fluency and voice. The three chapters of the second section will deal with the more subtle language disorders, which are of particular relevance during the years of schooling, since they interfere in the academic progress of these apparently typically developing children. In the final section, I will introduce the more grossly handicapping communication disorders which have far greater implications for the child's overall development including schooling and long term outcomes. Chapters 8 and 9 will cover children with hearing impairment and mental retardation, respectively. Chapter 10 will focus on the child with cerebral palsy. The next chapter deals with the variety of the Autistic Spectrum Disorders ranging from those which are mild in nature to those which are of late onset such as the Asperger's syndrome. The final chapter introduces and discusses other neuropsychiatric syndromes in children, which are accompanied by communication disorders.

At the end of the book a selected reading list is given. There are a great number of books on communication disorders in children that have been published in the West. However, given the cost of these books they are seldom accessible in India, except at national institutions. As a result of the recent changes in policy and social attitudes and the increasing emphasis on mainstreaming and integration of children with disabilities in regular schools, several Indian books on this topic are now emerging. The reading list given at the end of this book lists these as well as available Indian editions of Western books that can be accessed by the interested reader seeking more information.

Section I
Speech Disorders

Human communication is a complex process involving two or more persons. The terms 'communication', 'language' and 'speech' are frequently used in the context of human communication. While there is some overlap between these terms, there are also important distinctions between them, which need to be understood when dealing with children with communication disorders. Communication is a broad term that encompasses all forms of communication including the verbal and nonverbal. Verbal communication refers to the form of communication that all of us are most familiar with, that is communication through speech, and is often used to encompass a secondary mode, that is, the written mode too. Nonverbal communication can be of many different types including sign language, mechanical communication systems such as Morse codes and other communication systems such as those used by animals.

For verbal communication to occur it is important that the speaker and listener share a language, i.e. they share a common code or set of rules which govern the particular speech sounds they produce and perceive, and the rules that govern the combination of these speech sounds in to words and sentences. Without this common code or set of rules, or shared language, communication cannot occur. Human verbal communication thus constitutes two major components that is, the production, transmission and perception of speech sounds and the knowledge and application of a set of rules that governs them, that is the rules of the particular language that they speak. While speech is necessarily dependent on the oral-aural primary mode of communication, the rules of the language hold for other modes of communication such as reading and writing too. Thus, while speech is an integral part of language, language encompasses speech as well as other alternate modes of communication such as sign language.

The most common mode of communication that we use is often the first learnt or primary mode, which is also referred to as the oral-aural mode, that is, the speaking-listening mode. In this mode, the communication process begins with the speaker having a thought that he would like to share with the listener. The thought then has to be converted to language, that is, words and sentences. For these sentences and words to be expressed, the speaker has to produce a series of speech sounds. Speech is the spoken medium of language. The term 'speech' refers to the process of producing the sounds necessary for verbal communication. This process of speech sound production begins with an activation of a stream of air from the lungs. The vocal cords act on this stream of air by vibrating while it flows through them, and then on to the resonating chambers of the mouth and nose. While it flows through these resonating chambers it is further acted upon by other vocal organs such as the tongue, jaw and lips to produce a distinct set of sounds, which are the phonemes or speech sounds of a particular language. These speech sounds are perceived as a series of acoustic events by the listener's ears, which in turn, pass them on to the higher centres in the brain where they are perceived and identified as a set of speech sounds, which make up words and sentences that carry meaning.

The first milestone of normal speech is the birth cry, which when delayed can be an indicator of everything not being quite right. Within 2 to 3 months the mother is able to distinguish the cries of her baby as being indicative of hunger versus discomfort, a stage known as differentiated crying. The infant also responds to adult attention by cooing. From 3 to 6 months the baby starts babbling, initially in a random fashion and gradually rhythmically.

By 6 to 11 months babbling turns to imitative babbling, from which emerges the first word. A typically developing child will learn to say one or two words intentionally with reference to specific objects or people, by the age of one year. By 18 months the child will expand his vocabulary to about twenty words and this heralds the beginning of speech-language acquisition, a process that is spread over several years. When a child does not go through these stages of speech acquisition at the right time, a delay in speech acquisition can be suspected.

In older children and adults when a person is unduly concerned about his speech and avoids communicating with others, or when speech is considerably different from that of others of the same age, sex, or ethnic group, or is hard to understand, a disorder may be suspected to be present. A speech problem can be mild, moderate, or severe. Speech and language are composites of several factors and have different aspects, which may be selectively affected. Speech for instance has at least three major aspects, those of voice, articulation and fluency.

Voice refers to the result of the act of phonation that takes place as the air stream from the lungs passes through the glottis or vocal folds, setting them into vibration, resulting in different types of phonation such as voice, whisper and falsetto. Articulation refers to the production of the speech sounds of a language by vocal organs such as the larynx, pharynx, velum, nasal air passage, palate, teeth, tongue, jaw and lips that act in tandem to affect the passage of the air stream in various ways and at various points to produce the array of speech sounds that we use. Fluency refers to the ease with which the words flow, one after the other, without too many pauses, hesitations, repetitions and interjections and without disrupting the communication interaction.

The three chapters in this section will define and describe these basic aspects of speech and their development in children. This will be followed by a description of the commonly found speech disorders in children, under the categories of articulation, voice and fluency. Articulation disorder refers to problems in the production of speech sounds. The term, voice disorder, refers to problems with the pitch, volume or quality of the voice. Fluency disorders or dysfluencies are characterised by an interruption in the flow or rhythm of speech, such as in stammering or stuttering. It must be remembered though that while each of these aspects are described individually, two or more aspects of speech may be affected in the same child. Speech disorders associated with specific conditions such as cleft palate, cerebral palsy, cranio-facial anomalies, hearing impairment, paediatric stroke, traumatic brain injury (TBI), Down syndrome, and other syndromes and developmental disabilities, often have more than one of these components affected.

Assessment and management procedures for each subgroup of speech disorders will be described briefly. These generally include a case history, hearing and speech evaluations. Other evaluations such as an IQ assessment may also be recommended. Therapeutic intervention for these disorders is offered by SLPs. Children with articulation disorders are trained in the proper production of speech sounds. Children with voice disorders are trained to develop proper control of the vocal and respiratory systems for correct voice production. Children who are dysfluent are trained to reduce their dysfluencies and increase the amount of fluent speech and their confidence in their speaking abilities. The nature and duration of therapy will depend on the type and severity of the speech disorder. Each of the chapters will conclude with suggestions for a course of action if a child is suspected of having any such disorder, including home and classroom management strategies.

2

Articulation Disorders

We speak by making a series of speech sounds that are combined into certain patterns that make words. The speech sounds of a language are not produced a hundred per cent identically by all speakers of that language. Yet for speech to be acceptable and understood there should be enough similarities that each time a speech sound is produced by a speaker, all speakers of that language are able to identify it as representing that particular sound. Children learn this process of replicating the speech sounds of their language over a period of a few years, in early childhood.

Definition

Articulation refers to the correct production of the speech sounds of a language. The speech sounds of a language are its smallest indivisible units and are technically referred to as phonemes. The languages of the world draw from a small repertoire of about 60 phonemes to form the subset of phonemes that characterise each language. Each language has its own distinct subset of phonemes. The number of phonemes in different languages varies. All languages have vowels and consonants but the specific subset of phonemes and the manner in which they are combined to produce words differ from language to language.

All children irrespective of culture, creed and race acquire the speech sounds of their language (the language that they hear spoken around them in infancy) in a gradual fashion, spread over a few years, from birth or early infancy through the preschool years. This process occurs naturally and does not need any special instruction except in the case of those with some kind of anomaly. When a child does not acquire these speech sounds like his peers or produces them in a different manner then he will not be understood and he is considered to have an articulation disorder.

Incidence and Prevalence

Articulatory disorders are among the most common speech-language disorders. About 3 out of 5 of all speech and language disorders are said to be related to articulatory problems. 5–8 per cent of children entering school are reported to have an articulation disorder. The prevalence decreases considerably as the children get older and by primary school it is generally seen in 2 to 3 per cent of children and continues to decrease with increase in age.

Characteristics

Speech production is the result of a complex interaction between the respiratory, phonatory and articulatory systems. When a speaker decides to speak, neuromuscular activity sets off muscular action in the respiratory system producing a stream of air, which sets the vocal cords vibrating while passing through them. As the air stream emerges through the oral and nasal cavities the articulators act upon it by constricting in various positions and manners resulting in the production of a range of speech sounds. The vocal organs involved are the vocal cords, the larynx, pharynx, velum, nasal air passage, palate, teeth, tongue, jaw and lips. These vocal organs or articulators affect the passage of the air stream in various ways and at various points to produce the array of speech sounds that we use. For instance, in the production of the vowel 'aa' the air stream is relatively undisturbed as it flows through the mouth and out of the lips without any major obstruction. For the production of /t/ on the other hand the air stream is obstructed by the tongue, the tip of which is lifted up to the palate obstructing the path of air as it passes out of the mouth. For the nasal /n/ on the other hand the air stream passes through the nose or nasal passage instead of the mouth.

The term articulation refers to the process of speech production with varied placement of the speech organs such as the tongue, lips and teeth, which are referred to as articulators. Articulation deals with the production of the phonemes of the language, by the coordinated participation of the articulators, some of which are active and others passive. Active articulators are the vocal organs such as the tongue that move while passive articulators are the non-moving vocal organs such as the palate. Phonemes or speech sounds are produced when the active articulators come into contact with the passive articulators in different postural combinations while the air stream moves through them.

The mastery of articulation is a gradual process from early infancy to the early school years. By and large, the child masters the production of the sounds of his language, and their various combinations by the seventh year. This development follows a certain pattern – first the vowels, then some consonants like the bilabials m/b/p, which are relatively easy to produce, then come the other stop consonants, the laterals, fricatives, and sibilants, followed by mastery over complex combinations of these sounds. Clusters of phonemes where two or more consonants combine together, such as /tr/ in 'train' or /spl/ in 'splash' are more difficult to produce and are mastered late. Interestingly children follow the same overall sequence across the world, depending of course on the phonemes that exist in their language.

Western studies generally report that the typically growing child masters the correct production of all vowels and consonants such as m, b, w, h, n, t, d, k and g, by the age of 4 to 4 ½ years. This is followed by f, v, j, ng and l by 5 – 5 ½ years; s, z, sh, th and c, by 6 years and r by 7 years. There is general consensus that by 7–8 years a typically growing child is able to produce all the phonemes of his language accurately. Indian children learning English are reported to produce most vowels and consonants by 4 years of age and clusters of sounds by 6 years of age. Indian children learning to speak Indian languages master the production of the aspirated consonants, a little later, by the age of 6 ½ years.

When a child fails to produce a speech sound correctly because s/he cannot place the articulators correctly, it results in a 'misarticulation'. These articulatory errors can be due to a developmental delay or a disorder. When a child's articulation development is below his chronological age (CA) and he fails to acquire the adult articulatory pattern for the phonemes of his language, at about the same age as his peers, then it is termed as an articulatory delay. It may also be termed as an articulatory immaturity. The child often overcomes these articulatory delays with maturity and/or therapy.

Articulation Disorders

When a child acquires the speech sounds in the same stages as his peers but at a slower rate the phenomenon is known as an articulatory delay. However many children have consistent and persistent difficulties in producing some speech sounds, that are not in consonance with a straightforward delay. These speech errors, which are caused by a variety of factors, are called articulation disorders. A child with an articulation disorder will use an easier speech sound for a more difficult one as in /lolly/ for /lorry/, drop some phonemes or speech sounds from a word, as in /coe/ for /crow/, or mix up the sequence of speech sounds in a word as in /efalant/ for /elephant/. Often the misarticulating child has a few such errors but will make these errors consistently, despite correction. Some examples of common articulatory errors are /lolly/ for /lorry/, /thool/ for /school/ /cath/ for /catch/, and / suus/ for /shoes/. Most of the common errors are related to the accurate production of phonemes such as/k/, /g/, /s/, /r/, and the retroflex /l/ as in the Kannada word */halli/*. Occasionally a child may also add extra phonemes to a word such as in /animamal/ for animal. At times the child may produce the correct sound, but in such an effortful manner that the sound is distorted. Misarticulations in children are generally characterised by the use of a simpler sound for a more complex or difficult to produce sound. The child often knows the correct target sound but has difficulty in producing the necessary articulatory movements, for the correct production of the target sound. As a result generally the production of the word though not accurate is by and large intelligible.

It must be noted that at times, depending on the speech community that a particular child comes from, he may use a form of articulation that is different from the standard, for e.g. an Urdu- or Hindi-speaking child saying /iskool/ is acceptable within that community, since in Urdu and Hindi, words do not begin with the cluster /sk/ and the speaker is following the phonological rules of his language in adding the 'i' in producing /iskool/. However the same would be considered a misarticulation if the child were speaking English. These articulatory patterns which originate from the cultural or ethnic background of the child should not be categorised as a disorder. In the identification and evaluation of articulatory patterns it is therefore important to take into consideration the cultural or ethnic background of the child.

In the past these errors of speech production were simply termed as articulation disorders. However, with our increasing understanding of the role of speech perception and its acquisition in the child's speech-language development, distinctions are now made between speech sound errors that are seen in spoken speech alone as against those which coexist with difficulties in speech perception. For instance a child says 'mat' for 'bat' but knows the difference between what these words refer to. On the other hand, a second child may be unable to do both, distinguish between these words when spoken by another, as well as produce it appropriately. While the former who has a disorder in speech production alone is described as having an articulatory disorder, the latter whose difficulty encompasses both perception and production is said to have a phonological disorder. The latter is a more complex disorder affecting language acquisition at a more central level.

The term 'phonology' refers to the sound system of a language. The phonological rules of a language demarcate the phonemes or speech sounds of that particular language and how these sounds fit together in words. Phonological disorders are seen when a child has not correctly acquired the phonological rules of his language – the sound system and rules for sound combination. The child often simplifies the system or rules and consequently is unable to produce speech sounds in a manner that is age-appropriate. As a result his speech becomes unintelligible, often his parents being the only ones who can understand it. When a child has a phonological disorder, it is commonly found that other members of his family too had a similar problem. It may also affect the child's reading and spelling skills.

Causes

The majority of articulation disorders are developmental in nature, that is, children lag behind their peers in the correct production of the speech sounds of their language. For instance mastery of the retroflex / r / as in 'Rama' is difficult and happens around the age of 3 plus years. So if a 3-year old child is not producing it correctly it is not a major concern. But if a 5-year old is not, then it is of concern.

Children may also produce their speech sounds incorrectly because of the restricted or uncoordinated movements of their articulators. For accurate speech production the articulators not only have to move rapidly but also in a well coordinated manner. When speech sounds are produced in a deviant manner because of structural abnormalities such as those associated with orofacial abnormalities like cleft lips, or tongue ties, then they are termed as articulation disorders. Unlike an articulation delay a child is unlikely to overcome an articulation disorder without proper and sustained professional intervention. Speech sounds may also be poorly articulated because of poor speech models in the child's environment or because of encouraging/rewarding immature speech production as in lisping.

Depending on the likely cause, articulation disorders are classified as either organic or functional. Most articulation problems are not caused by any physical disability. These articulation problems are generally due to faulty learning and are referred to as functional misarticulations. The organic causes of misarticulation are many and range from a simple tongue-tie or misaligned teeth or dental malocclusion to more severe disorders such as cleft palates and motor coordination disorders. We will briefly describe some of the more common causes of articulation disorders.

One of the most common causes of an articulation disorder is what is known as a 'tongue-tie' in common parlance. In all of us the tongue is held or attached to the base of the mouth by a small band of tissue that lies midway beneath the tongue. In some children this piece of tissue known as the frenulum is either too short or is attached closer to the tip of the tongue interfering in the outward and upward movement of the tongue, thus tying the tongue too close to the base of the mouth. This restriction in the movement of the tongue interferes with the correct production of a set of speech sounds such as /l/, /t/ /d/ and /r/ and in the production of words which include clusters of these speech sounds. It must be noted however that frequently a delay in the acquisition of speech and language as a whole is attributed by laypersons to a tongue- tie. The fact is that tongue-ties, even the most severe ones, result in specific misarticulation and not in an overall delay in speech-language acquisition.

The lips too play an important role in articulation, particularly in the accurate production of those speech sounds known as the bilabials – the m/b/p and fricatives such as /f/ and /v/. On an average the upper dental arch protrudes slightly above the lower dental arch with the upper and lower lip gliding smoothly across these to meet in the production of bilabials, while the point of contact for fricatives is between the upper teeth and the lower lip. In many children these movements of the lips are interfered with, due to malocclusions or misalignments of the upper and lower dental arches resulting in what is known as overbite (when the upper teeth protrude more than normal) or an under bite when the lower teeth are in line with or even in front of the upper teeth ridge. These malocclusions often result in misarticulation of the concerned speech sounds. It must be remembered though that in a large number of cases with these kinds of malformations, the individual is often able to make compensatory adjustments that result in accurate production of the speech sounds. The articulatory process is fairly flexible and speakers can and do use different patterns of articulatory movements to produce comparable speech sounds, allowing individuals to modify their production of the speech sounds that are constrained by their physical structures, to some extent.

Cleft lips and palates are another category of anomalies with which some children are born. A cleft lip, also known as 'hare lip' refers to a condition in which a child is born with a cleft or a cut in his lip, usually the upper lip. This could be on one side of the lip or on both sides. Often the cleft extends backwards into the palate or roof of the mouth and occasionally all the way to the soft palate, with a missing uvula. Here too it could be on one side alone or restricted to either the hard or soft palate, or be extensive including both the hard and soft palates. Clefts known as sub mucous clefts, which are not visible to the untrained eye may also be present.

Cleft lips and palates are often surgically corrected in early infancy as they are very visible and more importantly they interfere in the feeding of the newborn infant. In some instances when the cleft is extensive, repeated surgeries may become necessary. At times when surgery is not possible, temporary aids such as prosthetic aids may be fitted. However, though the surgery and/or prosthetic aid may cover the gap in the oral cavity and aid in vegetative functions such as feeding, they are not always successful in providing adequate movements required for normal articulation. At times the scar tissue caused by surgery restricts the movements of the muscles involved, which in turn affect the articulation. Apart from the speech sounds that involve the lips, palatal sounds like /t/ and /d/ or velars like /k/ and /g/ can also be affected in children with cleft palates. Another overriding feature that is often seen in them is a nasal quality to their speech, which is caused by the inadequate closure of the oral from the nasal cavities, a consequence of the cleft palate. (This is dealt with in detail in chapter 3).

Yet another major category of articulation disorders are those caused by muscular in-coordination seen in children with conditions such as cerebral palsy or spasticity. Cerebral palsy is the result of a neurological insult to the brain often suffered before or during birth. These children have difficulty in producing smooth synchronised movements of the articulators as a result of which their speech can be slow and slurred or halting and staccato, coming out in bursts, depending on the type of cerebral palsy they have. Often the difficulties in speech are accompanied by other motor in-coordination as in gait and hand movements or even in vegetative functions such as chewing, sucking and blowing. At times the speech disturbance is so severe that the child is trained in alternate modes of communication such as pointing to symbols or letters and words or the use of speech synthesisers.

A related group of disorders caused by muscular in-coordination are the dysarthrias, which are similar to the cerebral palsies but not the same. Unlike cerebral palsy, which is seen at birth they are seen in children subsequent to some damage to the brain, as in head injuries or severe illnesses such as meningitis and encephalitis. The speech produced by them is slow and slurred and the difficulty is not specific to certain speech sounds, but affects all speech production. In the dysarthrias, the speech disorder is clearly due to paralysis, weakness or in coordination of speech muscles caused by central or peripheral nerve damage. In these children, slow and sluggish movements generally characterise all their speech with consequent poor intelligibility. They also often have drooling and difficulties with feeding. While some amount of spontaneous recovery may be seen, several have persistent and residual difficulty with speech.

In the recent past we are increasingly witnessing an articulation/ speech disorder, which is characterised by motor problems in positioning and sequentially moving muscles for the volitional production of speech. Known by different terms such as developmental apraxia of speech/ developmental verbal dyspraxia/ developmental coordination disorders, these difficulties are not caused by muscle weakness or neuromuscular weakness as in the cerebral palsies and dysarthrias. That is, even though there is nothing wrong with the muscles of the face, jaw, lips and tongue, the child is unable to coordinate his movements in order to produce speech sounds. A striking feature in this disorder is that the child often involuntarily produces these movements, but when specifically required to do so is unable to. The difficulties of these children in production of speech are thought to be due to difficulties in motor planning since they are unable to produce speech sounds in the absence of paralysis or weakness of the speech muscles. The quality of the speech deteriorates markedly when speech is demanded or the child is asked to repeat, with the quality of involuntary production being far better Consequently, the child may spontaneously utter a word or phrase but when asked to repeat the same, fails to do so. This is very frustrating for the child and his family as, in the case of the child he knows what to say but cannot say it and in the case of the family member it is perceived as being wilfully uncooperative. Yet the child's difficulty is a genuine one and in fact in some cases may be so extreme that at times the child is even unable to produce voice on demand. The child is observed to grope towards appropriate articulatory postures, often silently. The production of automatic speech as in counting or reciting the alphabet is far better than speech—the latter is often effortful and unclear.

Verbal dyspraxia often coexists with other types of subtle motor difficulties and the child is often seen as clumsy. Hence the alternate use of the term coordination disorder. Though unlike the cerebral palsies and dysarthrias there is no apparent neuropathology, DVD is seen more often in boys than girls and also tends to run in families, which suggests a genetic basis. Children with developmental verbal dyspraxia often require intensive and prolonged treatment. Speech therapy for this disorder involves improving planning, programming, storing, and retrieving speech motor patterns.

Misarticulation may also be present secondary to other more severe communication disorders such as hearing loss or mental retardation. In the absence of the acoustic input through hearing, the speech output of the hearing impaired child is often markedly poor in the quality of articulation. In addition partial hearing losses in children which selectively affect certain frequencies such as the high frequencies may result in their misarticulating speech sounds such as /s/ and /f/ which they are unable to hear. Similarly the speech of children with mental retardation may also show varying degrees of misarticulation that correspond with their overall language skills or are over and above their language delays.

Apart from the range of biologically caused articulation disorders, inadequate speech stimulation, poor speech models, encouragement of baby talk and exposure to two or more languages at a time may also lead to misarticulation. It must also be remembered that languages often have dialects that systematically vary the production of certain sounds in certain words. These are to be seen as dialectal variations and not as articulation disorders. There is also the influence of the native or the first learnt language on languages that are learnt subsequently. If the later learnt language contains a speech sound that is not present in the native language, speakers often tend to substitute a similar sound from their native language instead of the unfamiliar phoneme, particularly when the second language is learnt after puberty. For example, a Bengali speaker producing /van/ as /ban/ or a Tamil speaker pronouncing /Mohan/ as /Mogan/. It is also established that as the child grows older his ability to correctly perceive phonemes that are not existent in his language diminishes, resulting in a concomitant 'misarticulation'.

Articulation disorders are at times described by the kind of error the child makes in producing the desired sound – that is as a substitution error if the target sound is replaced by an easier sound as in wabbit/ rabbit, omission error if the child drops the target phoneme as in tain/train, addition if the child adds another phoneme as in galass / glass or distortion if the phoneme is produced in a distorted fashion, such that it becomes unrecognisable. The articulatory disorders are now classified more in terms of the process underlying the disorder rather than merely in terms of the type of misarticulation (substitution/ omission/distortion/addition). As described earlier, one of the more important distinctions of the type of articulatory disorder is whether the disorder is limited to expression alone and is one of misarticulation or a phonological disorder encompassing both speech perception and production.

Referral and Assessment

Any child with speech errors and particularly one who displays frustration or struggle when speaking should be evaluated at the earliest. For articulation disorders a referral is best made to the SLP who will study the child carefully and conduct the necessary evaluations. A speech evaluation generally starts by ruling out hearing impairment, followed by an oral examination covering the structure and movements of the lips, tongue, cheeks and jaw. Finally the child's production of the speech sounds of his language is checked individually and as a part of words in different word positions, as well as in continuous speech as in conversations and narrations. The SLP will also refer the child to other specialists such as ENT, plastic or dental surgeons if need be, prior to starting intervention.

Intervention

The first issue in intervention for articulation disorders would be to make an informed opinion as to whether a given child's speech requires further attention. This is fairly clear in the case of organically/biologically caused articulation disorders. The family would then have to consult with the family physician or concerned specialist such as the paediatrician, ENT surgeon/neurologist as the case may be. A second step would be to consult a speech-language pathologist in cases where medical intervention has not ameliorated the disorder. (A short list of available resources for these services in India is given in the appendix).

When there is no apparent biological/organic condition that could contribute to the poor speech of a child, since this is a developmental process, which changes over a period of time, a rule of thumb would be to determine whether the given child's speech clarity is comparable with that of his peers from the same socioeconomic, linguistic and cultural background. Alternately if a given child's speech attracts attention to itself rather than its content then it could be surmised that it is in all likelihood due to a speech problem. It is important however to give adequate consideration to the given child's linguistic and environmental background in doing this. If it appears that the child's articulation is influenced by poor models or because of exposure to other languages or to dialectal differences, then one could provide the desired model and observe the child for a period of time to ensure that the error pattern is not a persistent one. If on the other hand, the child shows specific and consistent patterns of errors on speech sounds that he ought to have mastered well by then, a referral to the appropriate specialists is called for.

Speech correction for articulation disorders is always carried out after ruling out medical/surgical intervention. So, for instance, in the case of the child with a tongue-tie the first step is to check the possibility of releasing the tongue-tie surgically, to be decided by a paediatric/ENT surgeon. Where this is possible it would be the first step in remediation and often the surgical release would enable the child to produce accurate production of the affected speech sounds. In some cases, either because of inadequate tissue in the frenulum for a release, or because of habituation, the disordered pattern may still persist. Then the SLP steps in to correct the misarticulation through remedial training.

Prior to initiating therapy the SLP will on the basis of the assessment results, determine which , if any of the speech sounds that are misarticulated by the child are developmentally inappropriate, or should have been produced correctly by that particular age. These phonemes are then targeted in therapy in a developmentally hierarchical manner, i.e., those phonemes that are acquired early are corrected first, and those that are acquired later are corrected later. The child is trained in the production of the correct sound through several stages. First, the child needs to distinguish between the correct target sound and the erroneous form that he is producing. Once he identifies the correct sound that is modelled while listening, he is trained to observe and imitate the required articulatory postures through the aid of visual and positional cues, i.e., showing the child where to place his articulators such as the tongue and lips. Vibratory and mechanical cues such as feeling the vibration at the throat for voiced sounds are also employed as and when required. Increasingly, computer graphics and interactive games are used for these purposes. Once the child learns the correct production of the target phoneme, he is provided with intensive drilling since such practice is needed if the child is to automatise the correct production and use it in his speech in situations other than at the clinic.

At times broader patterns of misarticulation may be seen. That is, a child may be misarticulating a particular group or subset of sounds and this may be caused by a single underlying error. For instance if a child has difficulty in voicing he will say /pa/ for /ba/, /ka/ for /ga/, and /ta/ for /da/. When such patterns are seen, instead of using the developmental hierarchical plan for therapy, the specific underlying error, in this case the feature of voicing is targeted so that the entire subset of sounds will be corrected.

Misarticulations are easier to correct when the child is young, at the preschool and elementary school level before s/he becomes habituated to production of sounds in a particular manner. Some parents, teachers and therapists prefer to wait until the age when all speech sounds are normally mastered by a child, that is, up to 6–7 years. However therapy is more effective if started early, that is by the age of 3–4 years. Even when therapy is not prescribed it is important to monitor the child periodically to ensure that his speech sound acquisition is proceeding according to schedule even if at a slower pace.

The duration of therapy is dependent on the age and severity of the problem apart from other environmental considerations. As a rule, the younger the child, the easier and quicker the remedial process. When a misarticulation has persisted over a length of time, then the therapist has not only to ensure correct production of the particular sound in isolation but also across different sound combinations and contexts. Habituated speech patterns are not easy to break through. When the misarticulation has persisted over a period of time, then it is more difficult and time consuming to get the child to not only master correct production but also to generalise, that is, to produce it involuntarily without conscious effort. It is here that the child's teacher and family can play an important supportive role in the therapeutic process, by drawing the child's attention to the need for conscious correct production across his daily life situations and to reward him for every such effort, thus ensuring that the correct pattern is firmly established in his spontaneous speech.

It is now increasingly clear that children with spoken language problems are at higher risk for literacy related problems. Not all children with articulation problems will end up having difficulty with learning to read and write. However those with phonological disorders and developmental verbal dyspraxia are particularly at higher risk for subsequent disorders of reading and writing. Given the increasingly obvious connection between phonological disorders, and literacy skills, it is important to monitor the acquisition of reading and writing skills in these children. Therapy for articulation, particularly in children with phonological disorders and verbal dyspraxia will additionally support their emergent literacy and strengthen a potential area of weakness. It is therefore recommended that these children are given intensive speech therapy at an early age to pre-empt difficulties with literacy acquisition. Most of these children benefit from speech-language intervention.

School Support

Apart from providing classroom and school support to the child during and after the therapeutic process, the teacher has a further responsibility in monitoring the child over an extended period of time. Children with articulation disorders are often seen to have additional difficulties in terms of poor auditory processing (despite normal hearing), poor auditory discrimination and auditory sequential memory, all of which are exacerbated in noisy surroundings such as classrooms. A sizeable number of young children who show up with articulation disorders in early childhood eventually exhibit signs of more pervasive communication disorders such as specific language impairment (SLI) or learning disabilities

(LD) such as dyslexia or specific reading disability. This would necessitate long-term monitoring of the child even after the articulation disorder has been resolved.

Parental Support

Parents are an integral part of any therapy programme for a child with a communication disorder. The first step that the parent has to take is to acknowledge that his or her child's immature speech pattern is not 'cute' and if not corrected can impede his overall learning and social skills. The correction of an articulation disorder is generally modelled and taught by the clinician in a clinical setting. In order for this achievement to be consolidated and converted into a long lasting gain in terms of clarity of every day speech, the teacher and parent have to provide the child with the necessary drilling support, in the stages worked out by the therapist. This will require the preparation of material suited to the individual child's needs in terms of practice word lists and extensive practice on the same. Once the child is able to produce the correct sound in the controlled situation of the clinic, the parent plays an even more important role in generalising or ensuring that this mastery is maintained across a variety of speaking situations by careful monitoring and providing positive support until such time as the correct speech patterns become automatised.

3

Voice Disorders

Of all the components of communication in humans, thc voice is distinctively individual, as personal and individualistic as our finger prints. It is as much a part of our individuality as our facial features. No two human voices are the same. It would therefore not be an exaggeration to state there are as many distinct human voices as there are human beings. However, within this enormous range, human voices can be grouped into some categories such as young versus old, or male versus female, based on some commonly accepted parameters. It is also true that while each of us retains a distinctive voice throughout our life span, each individual voice does undergo some changes through the different stages of life from infancy to old age.

Definition

Voice is a major aspect of speech production and occurs as the air stream passes through the vocal cords, setting them in vibration. During the normal production of voice the vocal folds vibrate regularly producing a smooth vocal tone that is perceived as a pleasant voice. At times this smooth production of voice is interfered with due to some abnormalities in the movements of the vocal cords. When the quality, pitch and loudness of a voice differs significantly from that which is customary in the voices of others of the same age and sex, it is classified as deviant or defective and described as a voice disorder. Voice disorders are seen frequently in children and can be corrected within relatively short periods of intervention.

Incidence and Prevalence

Voice disorders or dysphonias are fairly common in children. The prevalence reports vary from about 7 per cent to as high as 40 per cent. They are generally found to be higher among boys as compared to girls. The causes and types may vary at different ages. In younger children aged six to ten years voice disorders are often caused by vocal abuse or misuse, whereas around puberty they are related to the structural changes that occur in the body. It has been documented that the prevalence of voice disorders decreases in post-pubertal children.

Characteristics

The quality of voice is related to its pitch, loudness and resonance. These change from infancy to adulthood and then again in old age due to the structural changes that occur in the development and decline of the human body. They also differ in males and females.

As a rule, with a few exceptions, we are able to infer the age and sex of an individual by merely listening to his or her voice. Babies, children, adolescents, adult men and women as well as older men and women have distinctive voice characteristics, which differ from one another enabling us to categorise the speaker. The characteristics of voice also differ from one individual to another, again enabling us to identify the speaker, if known to us.

The recognition of voice is therefore also dependent on the listener's personal experience, which aid him in these judgments. When the voice characteristics of a given individual differ substantially from others of his age, sex and cultural background and draws unfavourable attention to itself, then it is classified as deviant or a disordered voice. Again, the impact of the listener's experience and background are factors that play into this process.

The birth cry of the infant is the first use of his voice and indicates that the infant is alive and respiration has begun. A delay in the birth cry puts the infant at risk for normal health and development. It is also now recognised that an analysis of the acoustic characteristics of the infant's voice, provide clues about the health of the infant and will help in early identification of pathological states. Distinct acoustic characteristics of the infant cry are now identified as indicative of a variety of disorders such as asphyxia, Sudden Infant Death or SID , congenital disorders such as Down syndrome, cleft palate, hearing impairment, central nervous system disease, metabolic disorders such as neonatal hyperbilirubinemia and low blood sugar, endocrinal disorders such as congenital hypothyroidism and even malnutrition

The most common early cries of the infant are hunger cries. Gradually a distinction between comfort versus non-comfort sounds emerges. By 6 weeks the infant starts cooing and from 8 weeks onwards infant vocalisation takes on characteristics of pre-linguistic vocalisation. Babbling begins by 3–6 months and by 6–12 months the infant's vocalisation is communicative. By this time the baby's voice is also individual and personal or unique to him or her. These early vocalisations of the infant are now being studied more intensively for they are recognised as providing a wealth of information on the emotional state, neurological condition, language acquisition and environmental influence on the child.

The quality of the human voice changes across the a person's life and much of this is related to the changes in the fundamental frequency of the voice perceived by us as the pitch of the voice. The infant's voice shows a rapid increase in pitch or fundamental frequency from birth to about 5 months. From then onwards it continues to decrease up to about 5 years and then settles. The range of the voice remains more or less constant between 6 and 16 years. From the ages of 10 to 16 years, along with the spurt in physical development, there is a sudden increase in the size of the larynx and the length of the vocal cords. Consequently, the voice drops in pitch. Additionally, due to the larger resonator of the larynx, pharynx and chest of the male there appears a clear distinction between the male and female voice around puberty. Voice mutation and vocal pitch changes seen at adolescence are related to these biological/physiological changes.

Voice breaks and pitch changes occur frequently among both boys and girls during these adolescent years. Generally they are not very dramatic or conspicuous. In some cases voice breaks are sudden and involuntary changes in pitch and quality are seen. These vocal shifts are a normal physiological feature of juvenile laryngeal function and are due to poor coordination of the laryngeal musculature associated with body growth. However they can be aggravated by vocal strain imposed by vocal abuse and result in voice disorders. Changes in singing voice go on for a longer period and should not be subjected to too much strain during the adolescent years.

Disorders

The quality of voice is dependent on the structure of the vocal folds and the function of neuromuscular controls. It therefore changes across the lifespan along with the structural changes that occur in the developmental process. Poor respiratory patterns with uncoordinated movements of the thoracic and abdominal muscles will result in excessive laryngeal tension. Crying brings about changes in the respiratory patterns and provides the necessary preliminary exercise for voice production. However too little crying, such as in a child who is constantly on a pacifier or too much crying leading to irritation of the vocal cords and eventually to vocal nodules, can cause voice problems.

The changing lifestyles of children that make them more sedentary, watching television, working on computers and being driven in cars; providing them with inadequate exercise, may affect respiratory patterns, air inflow and phonation. Physiological factors such as an immature and constantly changing larynx can result in a voice, which is lower in intensity and higher in pitch, has a small range and poor resonance. Strained phonation can also be the result of a child struggling to compensate for a low voice.

Voice disorders are characterised by abnormal vocal pitch, loudness, quality or resonance. The pitch may be too high or low or monotonous, that is never changing. When the pitch of a boy's voice is too high he will sound like a girl. On the other hand when the pitch of a girl is too low she will sound like a boy. It may be too loud or too soft. The overall quality may be poor, sounding harsh, hoarse, breathy or nasal.

Causes

Voice disorders occur when a child exhibits a deviation in the pitch, intensity, or duration of his/her voice. Children suffering from voice disorders often display a hoarse, raspy vocal quality and may have difficulty varying the volume of their voice and these are commonly referred to with descriptive terms such as 'hoarseness', 'raspy voice', and 'weak and breathy voice.' Often this is a result of overuse of their voice or talking too loudly. This phenomenon termed 'vocal abuse' is the result of excessive screaming, frequent coughing or throat clearing, or speaking at an uncomfortable pitch. When this behaviour persists for a prolonged duration, physiological changes such as 'callusing' or thickening of the vocal folds can occur eventually leading to vocal nodules. Some clinicians point out that vocal nodules are not merely the result of vocal abuse in a vociferous child. They suggest that this is too simplistic a view and that these children may have other emotional and behavioural issues such as anger and frustration rather than just being exuberant and extroverted.

The majority of young children with voice problems are found to have vocal nodules consequent to vocal abuse. In a smaller percentage this could be due to chronic laryngitis.

Allergies resulting in frequent coughing and throat clearing, as well as mouth breathing resulting in the drying out of the vocal folds may also lead to voice disorders. Acute dysphonia or sudden and total loss of voice is often caused by acute respiratory infection, which exacerbates chronic laryngitis. Often these children also develop a fast rate of speech.

Some children may be born with other kinds of vocal pathologies such as a vocal fold web or an inflammation of the vocal cords due to reflux disorders. Vocal fold paralysis or immobility is more common in adults and are seldom seen in children. Other conditions such as a hearing loss or a cleft palate may also contribute to a voice disorder. Children with a hearing impairment and poor auditory discrimination often tend to speak too loudly to compensate for these difficulties resulting in a strain on their voice. Similarly children with cleft palates and poor articulation and resonance may raise their voices to reduce nasality and achieve greater speech clarity, but affecting their voice in the process.

Nasal obstructions such as in children with a deviated nasal septum or damage to the larynx as a result of injuries and accidents can also lead to a voice disorder. Children with neurological conditions such as cerebral palsy and endocrinological disorders such as myxoedema often have consequent voice disorders. Among the most common causes of voice disorders in children, however, are laryngitis, both acute and chronic.

Another type of voice disorder often seen in children, particularly in males is one that is related to the structural changes in the larynx that occur around puberty. While these changes take place in both boys and girls they are much more marked in the former. During the occurrence of these changes in the size and volume of the vocal cords, the pitch drops considerably. The transition phase is often accompanied by pitch breaks with perceptible changes occurring frequently, at times even within the production of a single utterance. Boys who are unable to make this transition smoothly, often persist in the use of their pre-pubertal voice resulting in a condition known as puberphonia. In lay terms this refers to the inappropriately high pitch of a post-pubertal male (making him sound like a female). In contrast some girls adopt a pitch that is too low for their gender – a condition that makes them sound like a boy and is known as androphonia.

Performers such as actors and singers, among children, are at added risk for voice disorders due to the special demands made on their voice. They are also the ones who need to be trained in vocal hygiene at the earliest so as to enable them to pursue a career in these areas if they so desire.

Voice disorders as described above may occur in isolation or in combination with other speech and language difficulties impairing the child's communication skills further. It is important to remember that an isolated voice disorder may also be the result of more than one contributory factor and that these factors often blend and interweave in the causation and maintenance of a voice disorder. Most of the dysphonias or voice disorders seen in children can be treated successfully, particularly if identified early and provided with intervention.

Referral and Assessment

One of the first steps to be taken in the management of a voice disorder is a referral to an otolaryngologist or an ear, nose and throat (ENT) doctor. This is to be done prior to his being treated for the voice disorder by an SLP. If a child has a voice which is chronically hoarse, harsh, breathy or of poor quality, or if the voice is too loud or soft, or the pitch is either inappropriate for the child's age and sex and breaks frequently, or if the voice is hypo (lesser than required) or hyper (more than required) nasal, then the child should consult an ENT surgeon preferably in a specialist voice clinic setting. Persistent difficulties in keeping food and drink in mouth, chewing and swallowing, are also adequate reasons for a consultation with an ENT surgeon. The otolaryngologist will examine the child's mouth and throat to determine if vocal nodules or any other such vocal abnormalities are present and advise medication or surgery if required.

The SLPs intervention is carried out after the clearance from the ENT surgeon so as not to exacerbate any organic condition, if it exists. The SLP will assess the voice characteristics of the child to determine the type of voice disorder and if possible its cause, prior to beginning intervention. This begins with a detailed case history that takes in to account the history of the disorder and the vocal routine and environment of the child and is followed by observation of the child's respiratory patterns and characteristics of his phonation. Much of the assessment of voice involves perceptual judgment by trained clinicians, of the appropriateness of the child's habitual voice to his age and sex.

There exist a few perceptual scales for describing a given individual's voice characteristics. However, there is no general agreement on the terms that are used to describe voice characteristics or their application in specific instances.

Instrumental evaluations are at times carried out in the larger, better established voice clinics, but are not a must. The most commonly used instrumentation procedures are laryngoscopies to evaluate the appearance, structure and functioning of the vocal cords, laryngographies to provide visual outputs that reflect the functioning of the vocal cords, vocal tract imaging for checking the functioning of the vocal tract as a whole, acoustic analyses through oscilloscopes and spectrographs for measurements of the acoustic features of voice, airflow and volume measurements such as spirometry and pneumography, nasal anemometry for measurement of nasal resonance and electromyography for muscle tone. These objective measures are seldom used independently. Instead, the results of the objective measures are taken in conjunction with the clinician's perceptual analysis of the given child's voice disorder. Often the instrumentation is also used in treatment as a part of biofeedback procedures.

Intervention

The SLP's assessment will indicate whether the child's habitual voice is appropriate to his age and sex. If they are, then all that will be required is to teach the child proper vocal hygiene including techniques on how not to abuse his voice. Vocal abuse is in fact the most common cause of voice disorders, particularly in children. It may not be out of place to state here that along with children, schoolteachers are also among the most frequent victims of vocal abuse and what is suggested for the child will also hold true for the teacher with a voice disorder consequent to years of vocal abuse or misuse.

The very first step in remediation of voice disorders subsequent to vocal abuse is instruction in the mechanics of phonation, along with an elucidation of factors that affect phonation such as tension, poor respiratory patterns, posture and other psychological factors. This first step is applicable to remediation of all of the voice disorders, with specific additional procedures applied for those where the voice disorder is not due to vocal abuse.

Remedial measures begin with an attempt to increase the child's understanding of how voice is produced and the factors that affect it, often through the use of pictures and models. Actual remediation may be preceded by a period of 'voice rest' if the child's voice problem is acute. The child is also sensitised to tension in the supralaryngeal region of the throat and helped to reduce it by coordinating breath or respiratory patterns with smooth and relaxed voice production. Instruction in patterns of good voice production at an early stage is not only effective in improving the child's voice but is also preventive in the long term and protects the child from developing the long term effects of vocal abuse, such as the development of vocal nodules and polyps. It is important to work out a regimen for the child that avoids or reduces vocal misuse and laryngeal irritants. Voice rest and a voice conservation regimen that actively reduces prolonged usage of voice, along with avoidance of exposure to irritants such as dusty environments and particular kinds of food and drink can go a long way in reducing the risk for the long term ill effects of vocal misuse. Excessive loudness too can be harmful for the child and when this is the case, appropriate measures to reduce the same are initiated. Voice disorders in children may also be caused by habitual use of a pitch that is not best suited for the child. If a child is found to be using a pitch that is not best suited for him, then he is trained to recognise this, produce a pitch that is more appropriate to him and habituate the same. Respiratory exercises such as improved breathing techniques and relaxation techniques play an important role in voice therapy and are aimed at the facilitation of improved vocal function.

Several specific techniques are used in voice therapy, ranging from biofeedback techniques to behaviour modification approaches. While the former employ the instrumental procedures described above, the latter are based on methods such as a reward system or negative practice to shape vocal behaviour. However it is important to consider the multiplicity of etiological variables including the type of personality that the child has and his social interactions with his peers in order to enable him to sustain the gains made in therapy and continue to produce a trouble free voice. Choice of therapeutic methods will be not be dependent on the condition alone. It would also have to take into consideration the age of the child, his ability to understand the principles of voice care and to cooperate with the therapist. In addition the therapist has to take into consideration other factors such as the psychological, cultural and family issues in planning a therapy program. When a dysphonic child fails to respond to therapy despite good cooperation from the child and family, it is essential to review the diagnosis with the consultant ENT surgeon.

School Support

Vocal abuse such as shouting and screaming are among the most common causes of voice disorders in children. If vocal abuse continues over a period of time, it leads to more permanent damage in the form of vocal nodules leading to a chronically hoarse and harsh voice. It is apparent that the nature of some activities at school such as team sports events, group singing and theatrical activities may contribute to vocal abuse and its consequences, unless supervised by a person who has some awareness and training in using the voice properly, during these situations.

Children at school should be trained and encouraged in the proper use of voice. For those with a history of voice difficulties, alternative strategies such as gestures and clapping, in order to draw attention to themselves and be heard, should be devised and permitted. Adequate and intermittent periods of voice rest should be planned and provided.

Adolescents who plan on careers that are dependent on trouble free voices or professions, in which a lot of demand will be placed on their voices, such as singing and acting, should in particular, be sensitised to the demands that are likely to be placed on their voices and the precautions that need to be taken.

Parental Support

In addition to the support at school, permanent changes in voice management can only be brought about with understanding and support from the family and its lifestyle. Large families and joint families are situations in which a child has to compete for attention. Practice sessions for breathing and relaxation exercises have to planned and monitored regularly. Implementation of changes acquired in therapy, in the home situation, has to be planned for carefully. Partnerships between family and therapists are a must for successful voice rehabilitation.

4
Fluency Disorders

Most of us hesitate, pause, repeat and interject 'hmmm' and 'ha…' when we speak, some of us more so than others. Generally young children show more of these disruptions than adults. Yet we are seldom aware of or bothered by these interruptions in the smooth flow of speech. However, with a few of us these interruptions happen so often or are so marked that it disconcerts the listener and disrupts the flow of communication.

Definition

The term fluency in speech refers to the smooth, effortless, uninterrupted flow of an utterance. In lay terms, fluency is sometimes used to refer to the competence of an individual in a language which in turn enables him or her to speak in a series of smooth, effortless, uninterrupted utterances.

When the smooth, forward flow of speech is disrupted by frequent pauses, hesitations, interjections, prolongations and repetitions, then it is described as dysfluent speech or disfluent speech. Though some researchers and clinicians make a distinction between the uses of these terms as being distinctly applicable to non-fluency within normal limits versus non-fluency, which is considered to be abnormal, most people use these terms interchangeably.

Individuals vary in how fluent they are and the fluency of the same individual may differ depending on the speaking situation.

All of us are dysfluent at times, to a greater or lesser extent. However when these interruptions in speech are consistently present in an individual, to such an extent that they interfere in the act of communication by drawing attention to themselves rather than the content of the communication, then they are labelled as 'stammering' or 'stuttering'. The two terms mean the same and the choice of a particular word is dependent more on geography, with the former being more popular in Britain and the latter in the United States of America.

Stuttering is a fluency disorder, which disrupts the fluency of speech and is characterised by speech sound prolongations, blocks or interruptions to speech and sound, word and phrase repetitions, for example as in, 'ssssame', 'tuh-tuh-tuh-table', 'good..good..good morning'.

While stuttering is the most common fluency disorder there are also other, less known fluency disorders, such as adult onset stuttering and cluttering which occur much less frequently than stuttering. As the name suggests 'adult onset stuttering' is acquired in adulthood often as a consequence of an illness or a head injury. It is also referred to as 'neurogenic stuttering'. Cluttering, on the other hand is a fluency disorder, which is characterised by excessive speed of speech affecting speech intelligibility, also resulting in a communication breakdown.

Incidence and Prevalence

Though all of us have perhaps met or seen a stutterer, in movies and on television, if not in real life, stuttering is not a very common disorder. In fact of all the communication disorders seen in schools, stuttering is the least common. It is generally estimated that about 1 per cent of the population stutters, the rate being slightly higher than 1 per cent for preschool children and lower than 1 per cent for older children or in the adult population. The incidence of stuttering is higher in children because a considerable number of children show signs of disfluency during the stages of speech acquisition in early childhood. In fact the phenomenon is so common that it is termed as 'normal nonfluency'. Stuttering, like most other communication disorders is also much more common in males than females, with a ratio of approximately 4:1.

Characteristics

The speech of children becomes increasingly fluent as they mature. Development of fluency is parallel to developments in speech, language and cognition. The child's speech becomes more and more continuous from the age of 2 years. The disfluencies reduce over time. Interestingly not only is there a reduction in disfluencies but there are also changes in the types of discontinuities that are seen. At the age of 2 years the child tends to repeat small speech units such as syllables, interjects speech output with exclamations, or revises his utterances. However over the next 2–3 years there is a marked reduction of these repetitions. Pauses on the other hand do not show a reduction at this age. Filled pauses, that are pauses during which the child continues to vocalise syllables such as 'hmmm' are common between the ages of 3–5 years and are found frequently before content words or nouns. As children get older the duration of their unfilled or silent pauses reduce rapidly in early school years and then more gradually during the rest of the school years.

The fluency of a child is affected to a considerable extent by factors such as continuity of speech, rate of speech, effort, rhythm and other physiological factors such as coordination and timing in speech. Other factors such as the linguistic maturity of the child and the complexity of the utterances, particularly grammatical complexity also influence fluency at a given time. The sex of the child is an important factor in that, as a rule, girls are more fluent than boys, particularly during these early developmental stages. In addition other factors such as whom the child is talking to and where, also has an effect on the fluency of the child.

During the period of speech-language acquisition in early childhood, i.e., from the ages of 2 to 7 years children often have difficulty in speaking and tend to hesitate on or repeat some syllables, words or phrases. These are periods of 'normal disfluency' that most children experience as they learn to speak. These disfluencies occur most often between the ages of two and five years and they tend to come and go, over several weeks, as the child goes through stages of language learning. About 20 per cent of all children go through a stage of development during which they encounter disfluencies severe enough to be a concern for their parents. The highest numbers of these disfluencies occur between the second and fourth birthday of the child and then they gradually decrease. The onset of the disfluency is usually insidious, beginning with repetitious speech which is common at this age. It is generally episodic at first, varying from day to day and situation to situation. Very few report a sudden onset of disfluency. Many preschoolers gain fluency within one or two years of onset, but about 3–5 per cent of preschool to school age children will continue to exhibit stuttering like characteristics in their speech. About 1 per cent of school age children continue to have a long term fluency disorder. It is needless to emphasise that the fluency disorder will restrict their educational, vocational, personal, and social life, considerably. By school age the characteristics of stuttering are more firmly established and often coexist with more complicated feelings about speech and stuttering.

Differentiating the normal dysfluencies from fluency disorders can be tricky but important. Most normal disfluencies are either repetitions of whole words, or pauses and interjections. Occasionally the normally disfluent child may repeat syllables like 'ele-ele-elephant', or hesitate or use speech fillers such as 'uh ..uh'. Fluency disorders such as stuttering, on the other hand, are characterised by multiple repetitions of a syllable, or prolongations of a single sound like 'sssssnake' or abnormal stoppages in speech with no production of sound. These children often have abnormal facial and body movements such as eye blinks, head nods and tensing of the neck muscles associated with their speech difficulties. Often a distinction is made between 'normal disfluency' and 'stuttering' based on the amount of disfluency. When the child repeats words frequently, i.e., again and again in the same utterance, or pauses too frequently and for too long it may interfere in communication. Listener reactions are also a good indicator of whether a child's speech may be termed normal nonfluency or a fluency disorder per se, i.e., when the listener's attention is frequently drawn to the manner of speech rather than its content then the child is more likely to be considered to have a fluency disorder.

There are some additional factors that need to be considered when deciding whether the disfluencies of a child are to be taken serious note of. Among these is history – past or present, of other members of the family being stutterers. A child with a stutterer in the family is much more likely to have more long lasting disfluencies than one who has a negative family history. Further, if the given child has had a history of, or continues to have a speech, language or hearing problem then the risk of him becoming a stutterer is higher. Additionally, dysfluencies that persist over a year are in all likelihood indicative of a fluency disorder.

Disorders

By definition, fluency disorders are a group of speech disorders in which there is an interruption in the flow or rhythm of speech characterised by hesitations, repetitions, or prolongations of sounds, syllables, words or phrases. Among the fluency disorders, stammering or stuttering is the most common. Stuttering develops in early childhood, persists into adolescence, often exacerbating during this time and continues into adulthood. In some individuals stuttering may spontaneously disappear by adolescence and adulthood. Even when it does persist, the severity generally reduces in adulthood. Apart from the frequent repetitions, hesitations and excessively long pauses and prolongations that are characteristic of early childhood stuttering, secondary characteristics such as facial grimacing, arm or hand movements, at the time of stuttering often develop in school age or older children. The child may now begin to avoid some words and speaking situations.

The severity of stuttering varies in a given individual across speaking situations, from day to day and across the life span. Nevertheless stuttering may be characterised as mild, moderate or severe not only on the basis of the amount of dysfluency but also depending on the type and nature of the dysfluencies, and the presence or absence of secondaries. In a child with mild stuttering, speech is characterised by simple repetitions with some possibility of tension in the facial muscles particularly around the mouth. Occasionally there may be stoppage of sound production or a rising pitch during a speech block. These disfluencies come and go and are seldom present all the time.

In a child with more severe stuttering there is considerable effort and tension present during speech production. Unlike the repetitions and prolongations that are characteristic of the younger, milder stutterer, the speech blocks are more complete and are present in most speaking situations. The child now begins to change words that he perceives to be difficult and often uses starters (production of extra sounds or movements that the child believes will help in easing speech) and begins to avoid speaking situations. As stuttering persists through childhood and adolescence the stutterer often develops other emotional problems. These emotional maladjustments are often the result of both listener reactions as well as the stutterer's frustration at his own speech. Embarrassment, guilt and anger often lead to the social isolation of a stutterer affecting his overall sense of well being, expectations and aspirations.

Stuttering like symptoms may also be seen in other organic disorders such as Tourette's syndrome and spasmodic dysphonia. However these are identifiable as being different from stuttering in terms of the nature of onset as well as other symptoms that are characteristic of them but not of stuttering.

While stuttering is the most commonly recognised fluency disorder there are other lesser known fluency disorders such as cluttering. A rapid rate of speech that is difficult to understand is the most salient characteristic of cluttering. The rate of speech is so fast that often several speech sounds tend to get dropped making the speech unintelligible. Further, individuals with cluttering have some difficulty in language as well as in organising their thoughts

Causes

The cause or causes of stuttering are not as yet clearly identified. There have been prolonged debates as to whether stuttering is caused by organic or specific biological factors or by psychological issues. Genetics, developmental delays or lags including delays in speech-language acquisition, neurophysiologic immaturity, family dynamics and over expectations have all been cited as possible causative factors that lead to stuttering. Stuttering may occur when a combination of factors comes together and may have different causes in different people. In the 1970s there was an emphasis on the environmental and behavioural or 'nurture' factors as being causative of stuttering. Since then there has been a greater stress on the organic or motor factors. The higher incidence of stuttering in families of stutterers has led to the singling out of genetic factors as being the cause. Often there are other family members who also stutter, or stuttered when they were children. It is now assumed to be due to an interaction between a physiological predisposition that children are born with and their environmental experiences. For instance there has been some research that suggests that children with stuttering may have difficulty in the planning and production of complex, lengthy utterances. In addition they may also be overly sensitive to their speech errors.

It has been suggested that dysfluencies that eventually lead to stuttering, occur when the demands on the child's speech exceeds the capabilities of the child. As described earlier, within a broad framework, children differ in the rate at which they acquire speech and language skills as well as other cognitive and motor skills. When the demands on a child either in terms of parental expectations or comparison with siblings or peers or even the standards that a child sets for himself are greater than his capacities at a given time, it is likely that his fluency will be affected. There is seldom a single straightforward cause for a child becoming dysfluent. Stuttering is often the net result of a combination of factors including the physical, linguistic, environmental and psychological.

While most stuttering is insidious and gradual in onset in early childhood, stuttering can occasionally be the consequence of emotional trauma or a neural insult such as a stroke or brain injury suffered later in life. Emotional or psychological problems are not by and large a major causative factor in the onset of stuttering. However, occasionally an individual may become dysfluent subsequent to an instance of emotional trauma. This is also occasionally true of some individuals on recovery from a major debilitating disease. In addition, dysfluency in speech may also be a concomitant of brain injuries including strokes. This kind of stuttering is called adult onset stuttering.

Referral and Assessment

It is now believed that early identification and intervention is the most efficient and effective strategy for preventing the dysfluency from turning into a chronic lifelong disorder. If a parent or teacher suspects a child to have a speech dysfluency, it is best to seek help as soon as possible. If the dysfluency persists for 3-6 months or increases in severity it is best to consult a speech-language pathologist. One must also be careful to ensure that the person concerned is indeed a suitably trained professional, as there is a wide variety of 'miracle cures' that are offered by self taught advocates.

Children suspected of stuttering must have a thorough evaluation by a qualified SLP. This diagnostic evaluation is carried out not only to identify the presence and severity of a fluency disorder but also to differentiate it from other similar fluency disorders and to rule out associated problems such as an articulation or language delay, which may co exist. This base line evaluation enables the clinician to select the most appropriate line of treatment.

Intervention

Treatment of stuttering by medication, particularly using anti-depressant drugs has been tried. Not only have they not been particularly useful, but they have also had significant side effects. While a few, very few, physicians continue to try medication for stuttering, the generally preferred mode of treatment is speech therapy and behaviour modification.

There are a variety of successful approaches for treating both children and adults. In general, the earlier the treatment is initiated, the better the outcome. The best prevention tool is early intervention. For very young children in whom 'stuttering' is not clearly established as yet, the SLP may prefer to work indirectly through the parents rather than directly with the child. Therapy with very young children involves work with parents as well as the child. Parents are shown how to create conditions at home that are conducive to increasing the fluency of their child by reducing the demands placed on the child's speech. Parents are advised to be good listeners without feeling pressurised to complete the child's utterance for him, to keep their own language simple and appropriate for the child's language level, to let the child feel unhurried by keeping the parent's speech at a reasonable pace and through appropriate body language and to encourage the child to take turns in conversation and build his overall confidence. If necessary a few demonstration sessions are held with the child and parents in a play setting to elicit and encourage more fluent speech from the child and enable the parents to continue these procedures at home. The child is monitored over a period of time to ascertain whether parental intervention by itself leads to an elimination or substantial reduction in the dysfluency.

Most clinicians prefer not to intervene directly before a child is 3-4 years old and/or within 6 months of onset so as to allow for spontaneous recovery. The preferred rule of thumb until recently was to defer treatment but initiate systematic monitoring, for preschool children below the age of 5 years, with a history of dysfluency for less than a year and with no other speech-language disorders. The rationale for this approach has been to avoid attention to the child's stuttering so as not to make it worse.

However there are other clinicians who advocate therapy soon after onset, so as to prevent the concomitant/associated symptoms of 'avoidance' and 'struggle' from developing. Their rationale for early direct intervention is to be open about stuttering with the child who stutters and to work directly on fluency. They also argue that intervention provided earlier is more economical in terms of lesser number of sessions required and overall long term effectiveness. Speech therapy is recommended for a child with clear dysfluency and is often more successful when initiated before the age of five.

Therapeutic success with school aged children could be more limited. Speech therapy for stutterers can be a long drawn out affair with remissions. There are no instant miracle cures. Often fluency within a clinical set up is established relatively easily. Speech clinicians can help stutterers – children, adolescents and adults gain significant fluency. Stutterers are not only taught ways to modify and change their dysfluent speech patterns but also deal with the feelings and emotions associated with dysfluency and gain confidence in academic and social interactions. These are achieved both through individual therapy plans and /or group intervention.

Treatment programmes for stutterers can be varied. In most treatment approaches, speakers are taught to modify speech-related behaviours in ways that reduce the occurrence of the dysfluencies. The preschool child is often not aware that his dysfluencies are a cause of concern. With the preschool child, therapy focuses on modelling relaxed speech with increased pause time and slower turn taking, along with building self confidence and esteem through an appreciation of positive attributes. In contrast the school age child is often aware of his stuttering and may even react to it negatively. It is important to sensitise these children to awareness that some disfluency is normal. Speech therapy in their case begins with an exploration of their stuttering behaviour in all its aspects – physical, social and emotional. Older children are taught to ease the tension in their speech musculature and produce more relaxed smooth and effortless speech, working through their speech dysfluencies rather than suppressing or avoiding them.

Children who stutter have been observed to have coexisting articulation and phonological disorders that need to be addressed. There is also growing evidence to show that they may also have difficulty in executing demanding language tasks and are described as having fragile language skills. Since speech production, of which fluency is the end product, is a complex task, in which the intention to speak, the content and form of speech, as well as its motoric output is an overlapping and finely coordinated task any delay or inaccuracy at any one level will affect the final output and make it disfluent. When there are other accompanying speech-language deficits, an informed choice is to be made as to whether all of the speech problems are to be tackled simultaneously or whether they need to be prioritised and dealt with, one by one. These decisions are informed by the nature and severity of the coexisting problems and taken in consultation with the parent. In all instances of therapy for children, parents need to be involved in the therapy program, monitor them outside the clinic and reward their progress.

In case of the older, high school children who have to cope with the consequences of their fluency disorder and its repercussions in addition to the difficulties that the teenager already faces in his adolescent years, therapy begins by targeting greater understanding and acceptance of the dysfluencies on the part of the stutterer. These are generally achieved by a careful observation and description of the stuttering behaviour, highlighting some of the characteristics which were possibly learnt to deal with the stuttering and eventually becomes part of the stuttering behaviour. Techniques that will make the dysfluencies less tense and more manageable are then introduced. Finally reduction of the fear of speech and avoidance of speaking situations are targeted.

Speech therapy for stutterers is often conducted in individual sessions of about 45 minutes, 2 to 3 times a week. At times, where possible, this is supplemented by some amount of group therapy. The duration of therapy varies from individual to individual and is dependent on the severity of the stuttering as well as the ability of the stutterer with support from his family and friends to generalise the gains made in the clinic, in his everyday life. Not all stuttering can be completely 'cured'. Even those that are technically 'cured' may suffer relapses. The best chance for 'cure' is when treatment is begun at an early age. With older children therapy generally tends to help the child coexist with his stuttering without adding on additional behavioural, emotional and social complexities.

School Support

Teachers can play a central role in the management of children who stutter. For children who stutter, a teacher's understanding and support can be crucial because of their particular difficulties in interacting with their peers. The first thing that a teacher with a child who stutters in her class, should do is to refer the child to a trained SLP and continue to be in touch with the SLP until the child gains fluency. If the child is a young preschool child it is best to discuss the issue with the parents and the SLP rather than pay any special attention to the child.

Most of us experience anxiety when talking to someone who stutters and are not sure of how best to react. Often this results in well meaning but inappropriate reactions that lead to the greater discomfiture of the individual who stutters. It is generally helpful to listen patiently to the child who stutters and keep your own speech calm and unhurried. Providing extra time to listen to him and pausing before you respond will make him less hurried. Slow and relaxed speech on your part can be very effective, far more in fact than asking him to slow down. A patient, accepting attitude and a reassuring touch or smile will go a long way in reducing his tension and struggle with speech. Being able to talk about the stuttering often reduces the fear of it, which in turn will increase the fluency. Where appropriate encourage the child to speak about his stuttering, within an accepting milieu. This will help in reducing the speech related shame and fear that the child may be experiencing. Being acutely aware of the speech difficulties but not being able to talk about it to a trusted adult can also induce stress.

Paradoxically enough, changes on the part of the listener are as important to reduction of stuttering as are attempts to change the speaking patterns of the stutterer. Listen carefully to the meaning of what the child is saying rather than how he is saying it. Use language that is appropriate for his level when addressing him. Ensure that he is listened to without too many interruptions and that s/he does not feel left out of the conversation. The teacher's appreciation of something that he has said particularly well will go a long way in boosting his confidence in speech.

Teachers are often confused about how to deal with a child who stutters when it comes to classroom activities that involve speech such as responding to the roll call, reading out aloud or answering questions. Should he be left alone or be asked to participate like everyone else? As with so much else in the management of stuttering, this too depends on the individual child. If the child is unconcerned about his dysfluencies, as many children are, it is best to get him to participate like everyone else. If on the other hand the child is likely to get anxious and upset, it is best to allow him more time to build his confidence. If the child is already being seen by an SLP it may be advisable to consult the SLP for the best course of action for a particular child. Talking to the child in private and pointing out the fact that all of us have dysfluencies some time or the other, getting him to observe you and others carefully and pick out occasional dysfluencies will demonstrate to him that his dysfluencies are all right with you.

Answering questions in class is a particularly tricky issue. You can make this easier for the child who stutters by instructing the class that they are to take their time and think carefully before answering the question rather than rushing it. The child who stutters can be asked questions that require short answers and he can be given his turn fairly early in order to avoid his building up tension. For the child who stutters having to produce speech or reading in a predetermined turn or according to a predetermined schedule such as the roll call may be particularly difficult as he is likely to build up tension in anticipation of his turn. The turn for the stuttering child is best given out of turn when he appears relatively calm.

Reading aloud in class is yet another thorny issue. Most children who stutter are able to read more fluently than speak, particularly with some practice. It is helpful to give the material for reading in advance so that the child has an opportunity to practise reading it. In case this is not so for a given child who stutters it may be a good idea to get the class to read in unison in pairs, at least for a while. This will enable the stuttering child also to read in class and build his confidence.

Teasing is a particularly traumatic aspect of a stutterer's experience. Encourage the stutterer to report on teasing. It may be a good idea to talk to the teasers and explain that teasing is unacceptable and at the same time discuss ways and means of dealing with it to the child who stutters. If the problem persists the help of the school counsellor may be enlisted, where available.

The suggestions given above are generally supportive and are targeted to facilitate the child's fluency in the classroom. There are also several well meaning suggestions that are offered by teachers in the belief that it will help the child but may in fact have negative consequences. Telling the child to slow down or relax is one of them. Slowing down the pace of conversation by checking your own rate of speech will produce this result without the negative consequences. Getting the class to listen to each other without too many interruptions, is a good way of controlling everybody's speech rate. It is not a good idea to draw attention to the stutterer's dysfluency by completing words for him, finishing his sentences or speaking on his or her behalf. At the same time do not insist that he speak, hurry him along or ask him to start from the beginning. Punishing a child for his dysfluency is a definite no no. It is important to avoid treating the child who stutters, differently. At the same time calling upon him to perform verbally in front of others or getting him to do particularly difficult tasks such as conveying messages should be avoided. As and when the need arises, discussing the stutterer's speech difficulties in an empathic manner, with his peers, would also help others in his class to handle his speech difficulties in an appropriate manner. These suggestions ought to go a along way in helping the teacher assist the child who stutters, in the classroom until such time that schools in India have an in-house SLP who can be consulted.

Parental Support

Parental involvement in the management of the child who stutters is crucial. Teachers and parents should have a shared understanding of the problem. All decisions about the management of the problem should be made jointly and parents should be encouraged to play an active role in the same. The suggestions made to teachers to use simple language while conversing with the child who stutters, to maintain adequate eye contact while speaking, to speak at a reasonable rate and not too fast, to ensure appropriate body language, to avoid interruptions while the child is speaking and also speaking for him but instead to allow him adequate turns in the conversation, hold good for the parents too. In fact it is even more crucial that parents observe these simple rules while conversing with the child who stutters since it is they who are likely to be the child's most frequent conversational partner. The teacher's assistance and guidance to parents of children who stutter, on these lines, can go a long way in easing the speech related pressures of these children.

Section II

Language Disorders

When children acquire a language in childhood, they do it rapidly with very little direct assistance or teaching from adults. This universal capacity of children to acquire language and the universalities across all human languages is now generally believed to depend on biological systems. The child's ability to acquire language is seen to be dependent upon neural systems that are genetically influenced to do so. There is therefore considerable clinical and scientific interest in individual differences in children's development of language and in the aetiology of impairments of language development in children.

The three chapters of the second section will deal with the more subtle language disorders. These language disorders are seen in children who are developing normally or typically, but have a particular deficit in acquiring one or more aspects of language. It is important to identify these subtle language disorders since they interfere in the academic progress of these apparently typically developing children. Among these language disorders, three sub-types that have been identified and described with increasing clarity in the recent past—Specific Language Impairment, Semantic-Pragmatic Disorder or Pragmatic Language Impairment as it is also known, and Learning Disability; form the focus of chapters five, six and seven. It is also increasingly recognised that though they are treated as three distinct disorders, there is a considerable overlap between the three with the demarcating lines between them blurring and merging, particularly as children with these language impairments grow and the communicative and academic demands made of them, change.

Language is a code that we learn in order to express wants and needs and to communicate. All human languages are characterised by some essential features such as speech sounds, which combine to form words, which in turn combine further resulting in sentences, narrations, stories, conversations and so on. All languages have sets of rules that govern them. Phonology refers to the study of the sound systems of language. Phonology deals with the description of the systems and patterns of sounds that occur in a language. In order to become proficient users of a language we need to master the phonological rules of the language which enables us to identify the phonemes or speech sounds of that language and sensitises us to the rules that govern their combinations. Syntax refers to the grammatical rules of language. The syntactic rules of a language determine how words can be arranged in a sentence to indicate the relationships between those words and the meaning of the sentence as a whole. Semantics refers to the study of meaning in language. It encompasses meaning not only at the word level but also at the level of phrases and sentences. It also encompasses our knowledge of the relationship between words, as for instance among opposites.

Language is also described as having content, form and use. The meanings of words can change according to their grammatical context or the manner in which they are said, as for example in puns and sarcasm. There are also rules that govern the use of language across social situations, across listeners, across contexts. The term pragmatics is used to refer to the set of rules that tell us what to say, as also how and when to say it. At the level of pragmatics there is a shift from language as a formal and context independent system as viewed by most linguists until recently, to a broader framework derived from a functional perspective of language, which emphasises the use of language in social contexts. It must be remembered that though these distinct aspects of language have been recognised and while it is true that substantial mastery of any one aspect occurs during particular phases of language acquisition by the child, all these aspects act simultaneously in every speech act and there is no clear cut division in their acquisition. The acquisition of one aspect bootstraps another aspect and a delay or disorder in the acquisition of one will affect the others.

Children begin to acquire their vocabulary by the time they are 12 to 18 months old. By the time they are two years old they have a vocabulary of about 50 words. At this stage they start combining these words into simple two word phrases. By three years they begin mastering syntax or the rules that dictate how words are to be combined into sentences. Between three and five years of age there is a rapid increase in both their vocabulary and their command over syntax. These are the years of the interminable questions – what, where, who, why and how. By the time they are five they are capable of telling a simple story. As they get older they master complex language use as in gathering and providing information or narrating incidents and increasingly become proficient in the social and information seeking functions of language.

The most common language disorder is a delay in the development of language characterised by a marked slowness in development. Language disorders may also be characterised by specific difficulties affecting any one or more aspects of language acquisition such as understanding, speaking, building and expanding a vocabulary, mastering the grammar or syntax, using language forms that are suited to particular social contexts, or understanding and using figurative language. Children with language disorders may have difficulty in one or more of these areas and could often demonstrate a significant gap between their verbal and nonverbal abilities.

Language disorders are further classified in terms of their specific characteristics. A major subdivision is between the receptive and expressive language disorders, depending on whether it is the understanding of language that is affected or the expression of language. A child who consistently confuses between similar sounding words like 'bell' and 'ball', or has difficulty in following oral instructions but overcomes them when there are enough contextual cues as to what is required, could have a receptive language disorder. Other children may have difficulty in retrieving appropriate words, rapidly enough, while speaking. Still others may have no difficulty in expressing their needs simply, but have difficulty in organising words and sentences when expressing more complicated thoughts and ideas, when describing, defining or explaining events or sharing information. These impairments in expressive language may also affect the child's play and social use of language, leading to poor peer interaction. These children with expressive language delays usually do not talk much or often. A 4-year old who speaks only in two word phrases, clearly has an expressive deficit. Receptive language disorders invariably have a consequence for expressive language development. The latter on the other hand can be seen in isolation. Often these disorders coexist. These relatively subtle language disorders often coexist with processing disorders such as auditory processing disorders (not hearing impairment) and deficits in memory and capacity loads. The receptive and expressive disorders could also selectively affect any one or more linguistic aspects of language such as semantics, morphosyntax and syntax, discourse, pragmatics and prosody. Here again a deficit in any one level will have its repercussions on the acquisition and use of the other aspects too. Language disorders may be restricted to reading and writing alone without spoken language being affected. These children may have difficulties with learning new information in school or in spelling, in using words correctly, or composing sentences and essays. Children with difficulty in speaking, listening, reading, and writing, often get very frustrated when they cannot express the idea they wish to communicate. They may become withdrawn socially because they cannot use language to relate to peers.

Language disorders may coexist and be causally linked to other speech disorders such as fluency and articulation disorders, as described in the previous chapters. Language acquisition is closely linked to social development and consequently children with language disorders are also likely to lag behind and have difficulties in social development as well. The prevalence of language disorders in preschool and school children is said to range between 2–8 per cent. The prevalence of reading disorders is said to be even higher.

SLPs utilise a variety of language assessments in order to determine whether or not a language disorder is present. Assessment of language impairment is carried out for receptive and expressive language separately and is generally designed to tap language skills at specific age levels such as infants, preschoolers and school-age children – primary and high, given that these skills are mastered in stages across a wide age range. Since the 1970s and 80s with the advent of the discipline of psycholinguistics, for the first time the skills of the psychologists and the linguists, were jointly applied in the study of language acquisition by children. Consequently, there is now a vast body of fine-grained knowledge on children's acquisition of language, though we are still a long way off from understanding the entire process.

As a spin-off there has also been considerable work on developing tools for the assessment of the many and varied aspects of language across children in a wide age range. This has in turn heightened our sensitivities to the presence of several subtle disorders of language acquisition in children, as also their consequences for cognitive and social development. What is increasingly becoming clear over the last couple of decades is that children could have difficulty in acquiring any one or more aspects of language and these deficits not only affect the overall communication skills of a child, but also his social and cognitive development, and that this complex interaction keeps changing further with age and the increasing demands on the child, often giving rise to behavioural disorders. It must also be remembered that the entire area of developmental language disorders in children is now in a state of flux with several subtypes identified, yet at the same time showing considerable overlaps between them. It is expected that with continuing research and documentation this state of affairs will clear up and a better understanding of the developmental language disorders emerge. One should not be surprised to find that some of the current labels may then be discarded or perhaps replaced by newer ones.

Intervention procedures for children with language disorders are also determined by the age of the child, differing from infants to toddlers to school age children and will range from pre-linguistic training to classroom – based instruction, using a variety of techniques and strategies. Therapy targets may range from vocabulary building and concept formation to complex language skills, as the child grows older. Since communication skills are at the core of education, support in the form of language therapy may be required for some children throughout their school years. Reading and writing may pose special problems. Language disorders are increasingly being recognised as underlying not just reading disability but also a wider range of learning disabilities including conditions such as ADHD, eventually affecting the psychological and social well being of the growing child.

In addition there are the considerations of the effect of social factors such as being exposed to and having to learn more than one or two languages. Bi/multilingualism is clearly of importance in considering whether a given child has language impairment. The numerous languages and dialects that coexist within small geographical areas in countries like ours merit special attention. They pose special challenges in assessment, diagnosis and intervention for children with suspected language impairments. We have to be innovative and logical in our solutions considering our particular socio-economic and cultural milieus.

Finally, for those who are unable to master the spoken form of language, alternate and augmentative communication systems are increasingly being employed, so that every child has some means of communication at his command. These may range from the gestural, such as the sign language to picture boards or communication boards to highly sophisticated technology based devices such as speech synthesizers. As we move through the twenty-first century the range and availability of AAC techniques will undoubtedly broaden. These are the issues that will be covered in the following chapters.

5

Specific Language Impairment

Language acquisition is a complex process that is not fully understood as yet. Though the potential to learn language is present at birth, the child needs to be exposed to and stimulated with language in order to learn it. Language is not taught to children and most children learn it without effort. However for a small proportion of children the process of language acquisition is not a smooth one. Even though their other development is normal and they have no specific abnormalities, such as a hearing impairment or mental retardation; they seem to have a particular difficulty in acquiring language in the same fashion as their peers. These children are considered to have a condition that is now termed 'specific language impairment' (SLI). The difficulty in language acquisition that these children experience continues to remain a primary concern as the child grows, and often persists right into adulthood.

Definition

Different people have defined Specific Language Impairment (SLI) differently, with minor variations in these definitions. For instance 'SLI is a developmental language disorder in the absence of frank neurological, sensory-motor, non-verbal cognitive or social emotional deficits', or 'the term specific language impairment is used to describe children who have problems with the acquisition of spoken language despite normal nonverbal ability'. The defining features of the disorder however are (i) a significant language problem, (ii) in children with normal intelligence and normal hearing and (iii) in the absence of sensory deficits, neurological impairment and psychiatric disorders and (iv) despite adequate linguistic exposure. SLI is therefore an exclusionary diagnosis or a diagnosis that is made by ruling out a series of factors that could account for the delay in language development. It is a 'pure language delay'.

Some researchers and clinicians advocate the use of the term 'SLI' to refer to only those children who continue to have significant delays in language acquisition even after the age of 4 years, preferring to use the term 'late talkers' to refer to those children who overcome their language difficulties by 4 years of age and show no significant delay after the age of 4 years. There are others who argue that SLI applies to part of a larger group of children who do not acquire language as rapidly as their peers and are referred to as having developmental language disorders (DLD). Other terms such as language learning disability (LLD) have also been used to refer to this condition. In the past these children were referred to as having 'developmental dysphasia'. However since the term 'dysphasia' implies some kind of neural insult or brain damage, it has been dropped.

Incidence and Prevalence

In Western literature, it is stated that SLI affects about 5 per cent to 7 per cent of all children starting school. The prevalence of SLI in school going children is estimated to be about 7–8 per cent making it a more common disorder than hitherto thought. Given its consequences for academic and social skills the impact can be considerable. Research on SLI in India has barely begun and we therefore have no comparable figures. Nevertheless there is no reason to believe that the picture is any different here. In fact practising SLPs in India are now seeing an increasing number of children with characteristics of SLI.

Characteristics

Normally a child produces his first word by the age of one year, builds up his vocabulary gradually between the ages of 1 and 2 years, which then witnesses a massive spurt. By 18 to 24 months the child begins to make rudimentary sentences by combining two words and over the next year, starts using short phrases of 2 to 3 words.

Between the ages of 3–7 years s/he masters much of the grammar of her/his language and starts making adult like sentences. The finer aspects of language such as its use in different contexts, for different social purposes, or the use of refined syntax for purposes of precise information exchange as in academic exercises and discourse, or the subtle play of language in humour and puns are gradually built over adolescence and adulthood. The language difficulties of SLI children could encompass this entire range of linguistic processes. However when SLI is recognised in early childhood they are more marked at the earlier aspects of language acquisition such as vocabulary and syntax and are manifested as vocabulary deficits and grammatical inadequacies. Children with more severe language disorders will show these delays, as well as difficulties in later learnt language skills such as spelling, reading, and writing and the more complex aspects of language involved in academics and discourse.

As is clear from the definition of SLI, language acquisition is the primary area of concern as the child grows and develops, and there are no obvious related causes such as hearing loss or low intelligence for the language delay. Since language learning is highly dependent on categorisation and rule learning, the difficulty of SLI children was perceived as a difficulty in rule induction specific to language tasks and syntax in particular. Since no difficulties were observed in nonverbal rule induction it was suggested that the rule induction deficit was specific to morphosyntactic patterns and are language specific.

Considerable research has been carried out on SLI in the last twenty to thirty years and as a result a clearer picture of the language deficits is emerging. It now appears that SLI which was once considered to be a primary deficit in vocabulary building and acquisition of grammar indeed has much wider ramifications in language acquisition, covering all four major domains of language acquisition—phonology, syntax, semantics and pragmatics, apart from deficient prelinguistic behaviour and attentional deficits. Their language profiles are often uneven leading to questions of whether SLI is merely delayed language acquisition or deviant language acquisition. In addition they have been identified as having processing deficits such as difficulty in interpreting rapidly sequenced auditory or visual stimuli and visual motor integration. Some children with SLI are clumsy and more accident-prone. Tardy fine motor and oromotor skills have also suggested that there may be a more general but mild neurodevelopmental problem.

At the phonological level, children with SLI follow the same developmental pattern as their typically developing peers but at a slower rate. In addition they may have some difficulty in mastering specific consonants particularly those in the word-ending position. They may have a tendency to speak softer and be less voluble than their playmates. Similarly in the acquisition of the lexicon or vocabulary too, they may be slower than their contemporaries and may have greater difficulty in repeating non-words or nonsense words and in learning new words. Unlike typically developing children, they do not start combining words into phrases until the age of 3 years, seem to have particular difficulty with morphological inflections and continue to produce ungrammatical utterances for a longer period than their peers. Their pragmatic skills are also slow to develop and they are less communicatively interactive than their peers, though this is not the most marked linguistic deficit as in those with pragmatic language impairment, which will be discussed in the next chapter.

It has also been proposed that the perceived difficulties in grammatical form may be due to an underlying difficulty in processing brief and rapidly changing auditory information. Grammatical markers are often very brief in duration and may pose special problems for children with such auditory processing difficulties. An alternate viewpoint is that these children have poor short-term memory for speech sounds. Good short-term memory is a prerequisite for and goes hand in hand with the acquisition of vocabulary and speech production and deficits in short, term memory could well affect language acquisition.

Subtle cognitive deficits may also be present in children with SLI affecting their use of gestures, symbolic play and touch perception. Impaired reasoning skills have also been cited. In the performance of complex or multiple tasks, SLI children fare poorly as compared to their peers. They have difficulty in processing rapid speech and tend to perform better when instructions are given slowly. This slowness is seen in processing mental tasks that involve auditory-verbal processing as well as other kinds of mental tasks such as mental rotation and memory for pictures. Their information processing skills on the whole appear slower than typically growing children of their age.

This wide range of difficulties has raised the question of whether these children have a general deficit in symbolic competence. However, by and large, the consensus so far is that these deficits are more in the nature of a quantitative deficit rather than a qualitative difference.

Disorders

Subtypes of SLI are identified based on whether both receptive and expressive skills are affected or whether the difficulty affects either one aspect exclusively. Some children with SLI can understand language better than they can speak. A two-year old may understand simple instructions but be unable to produce two word phrases to express his needs. A four-year old may understand stories but be unable to reproduce them even as simple narratives. They do not talk much or often, though they do understand much of what is said to them. As the child with an expressive language disorder becomes older he may have no problem in expressing simple needs but might have difficulties in choosing the right words and organising these words into sentences that convey complex thought and ideas. They may have difficulties in describing events, defining words and concepts, giving instructions, explaining ideas, and narrating events. In school-aged children, these expressive language difficulties may be manifested in writing as well, resulting in difficulties with spelling, using words correctly, composing sentences, and writing compositions. These children are said to have an expressive language disorder.

Others may have difficulties in both understanding and expressing themselves in language and they are described as having a mixed or receptive-expressive language disorder. In some children understanding or speech reception may be affected to a greater extent than expression, but they are generally more difficult to identify without formal assessment. Their main characteristic is the inconsistency in their linguistic performance. These children are at times also referred to as having auditory processing disorders (APD) or central auditory processing disorders (CAPD) since their difficulty in processing language consistently is seen to be caused by auditory processing difficulties of a higher order, than a peripheral hearing loss.

The severity of SLI may also differ from child to child. The child with severe SLI will tend to be identified early, as the delay in the acquisition of language will become evident in the preschool years itself. Their linguistic milestones will lag considerably behind their peers and will draw attention to it. In children with milder degrees of SLI, the disorder may not become evident until school age. When the child has to rely more on his linguistic skills in the decontextualised communicative environment of the school she may face difficulties in academic work that is highly dependent on language such as in answering questions, summarising information, narrating or writing reports and essays.

Cumulatively they will be seen as reading and learning disabilities in school. A fallout of these milder undetected disorders is an increasing frustration leading to either aggression or social withdrawal and at times to school dropout. Teachers' perception of these children is also likely to be affected as a result of these increasingly spiralling effects of the language disorder.

Causes

The aetiology of SLI is as yet unknown. Unlike other children with developmental language disorders that are caused by say, a hearing impairment or mental retardation, children with SLI are identified by the criteria specified for the diagnosis of SLI rather than the cause of SLI. Aetiological theories of SLI cover the gamut of theories of normal distribution, perceptual deficits, linguistic deficits due to neurophysiological deficits and familial factors including genetic factors.

At one extreme of the interpretation of the cause of SLI are theorists who argue that children with SLI are not a group of children with a disorder but represent those who fall on the lower end of the normal distribution curve, that is they are simply less skilled, representing the lower end of the normal distribution of language ability. Perceptual theories of causation of SLI, posit that the impaired ability to learn language is caused by a deficiency in auditory processing of the incoming speech stream. Linguistic theories have on the other hand argued that the underpinnings of the universal grammar in human biology are damaged in these children. There is some evidence that the neurophysiology of language processing is different in children with SLI. Neuro imaging studies using techniques such as MRI, suggest that the brains of children with SLI may be morphologically (structurally and functionally) different from normally developing children.

Environmental factors such as the communicative environment and the mother-child interaction have been ruled out as causative factors. However, familial aggregation of individuals with SLI and the higher incidence among twins has in the recent past led to a focus on inherited tendencies or genetics. The documentation of a higher than normal incidence of language problems in the extended families of children with SLI and the higher incidence of language impairments among identical twins has led to the study of SLI becoming the focus of the search for the 'language gene' in the last decade. The excitement of locating the disordered language gene is now more tempered with the growing evidence that while genes undoubtedly play a strong role, environmental influences cannot be ruled out. Further the specificity of the language impairment in SLI is increasingly being questioned as associated impairments in motor skills, cognitive function, attention, and reading are documented in children who meet criteria for specific language impairment.

SLI continues to be an active area of interest for researchers from diverse backgrounds who are interested in the neurobiology of language acquisition in the human child. It is now the focus of studies that use a wide array of tools and techniques such as neuroimaging (structural and functional) studies, neuropyhsiological studies of auditory processing using auditory event related potentials as well as genetic studies. Such continued research interest is likely to lead to a better understanding of the neurobiology of both specific language impairment and language acquisition per se, both of which are critical for the better understanding and management of this disorder.

Referral and Assessment

As with most other communication disorders, in SLI too, early identification and intervention are best from the point of view of reducing long-term difficulties. If a child does not start talking by two years of age, rapidly taking major strides in his language acquisition, making him an inveterate question bank by the age of four years and is instead struggling to make himself understood, it should be a matter of concern. It is true that some 'late talkers' grow out of it and become normal speakers, while others do not outgrow their delayed speech pattern and instead end up having a long lasting problem in language acquisition and communication. When a child is growing typically in all other areas but not in communication skills and does not outgrow his speech delay within the first few years of his life, SLI should be suspected. Many of these children present with an unremarkable developmental history.

The discrepancy between expected and actual language skills, when persistent beyond the age of three years, with normal motor and social-emotional development and in the absence of a hearing impairment or mental retardation, should alert an adult to the possibility of an SLI, particularly if there is a family history of 'late talkers' or others with communication disorders of other types. It has been documented that a 'late talker' without family history of 'late talkers' or 'dyslexia' is more likely to resolve his speech-language difficulties by the age of 3 to 4 years than one who has a significant family history of ' late talkers' and 'dyslexics' or 'learning disabled'. The ones with family history continue to have difficulties beyond the age of four years and often require professional help from an SLP.

A formal assessment by a qualified SLP will indicate whether in fact the language age of the child is out of tandem, both with his overall accomplishments and the language skills of his peers. Children with SLI are often not identified until around 4 or 5 years of age, though some may have had consultation with SLPs earlier in the preschool years. When intervention is provided early, several preschoolers with SLI do achieve successful remediation.

When the communication difficulties of a child with SLI persist into the early school years, some call it a language learning disability. Children with milder communication deficits may also not show signs of their difficulties until they begin to learn to read and write in school. These children are referred to as children with 'hidden' language disorders. In some other cases children whose communication difficulties had 'resolved' may show a relapse of their difficulties when their communication skills are put to the rigorous and more demanding tasks of academics. In some instances these difficulties may surface only under the even more demanding environment of the middle or high school when a high level of linguistic sophistication is required to perform tasks involving interpretation, reasoning and abstract thinking. These children may be identified as having a language problem only in middle or high school. However given that their language deficits are likely to impact their literacy acquisition there are long-term educational and social implications to be considered.

The term 'language learning disability' (LLD) has been introduced to refer to these children with subtle language deficits that affect their literacy acquisition and dub them as learning disabled. Their subtle language learning difficulties may become apparent only when faced with higher-level language tasks required for conceptual understanding in middle or high school. Here too, the language learning disability may be restricted to the receptive or expressive aspect or involve both aspects. However the language disability is a significant one. While it is not a must that all individuals with a language learning disability will necessarily have literacy problems, given the extent to which language and literacy are tied in, it invariably becomes so. The degree to which the language deficits affect an individual's scholastic performance can be determined by careful assessment by an SLP. The SLP along with parents, classroom teachers and other professionals such as resource persons and tutors can help these children find effective ways to overcome the effects of the language disorder by using strategies that are effective in facilitating learning and independence in learning.

Children with SLI and LLD require systematic language intervention over a prolonged period of time, given that language acquisition is a complex process that spans across several years. Even so, they often continue to remain less skilled in aspects of communication as compared to their other cognitive skills and achievements. Though they may not manifest significant language problems their functioning in language related tasks such as reading, writing and spelling are not on par with their other skills and may in fact remain below average.

Many, but not all children diagnosed with SLI in their early years tend to have specific reading difficulties in their school years. It is now evident that there is an overlap between SLI, reading and learning disability. SLI does affect a child's academic success, particularly if left untreated. In the Western literature it is stated that 40 to 70 per cent of children with SLI are reported to have difficulties in learning to read. The possibility of developing reading problems are said to reduce if the child is particularly strong in nonverbal intelligence. It is also becoming increasingly evident that many children identified as dyslexics have had a history of language difficulty in their early years, though they may not have been diagnosed with SLI at that time. It has been observed that children identified as having delayed or impaired language development have gone on to facing reading problems. This suggests that the two disorders are part of the same continuum. The nature of the relationship between the two is debated. It is also true that not all children with SLI become reading disabled and not all children with reading disability have had language impairments. We will return to a discussion of some of these issues in a later chapter on learning disability (chapter 7).

Intervention

The SLP plays a key role in the assessment and management of the child with language impairment during the preschool and early school years. Much of the intervention is direct at this stage with additional input from the parents under the guidance of the SLP.

The SLP may work closely with a multidisciplinary team of doctors, audiologists, psychologists and teachers as required by the needs of an individual child. As the child makes the transitions through different phases of school, the class teacher and resource teacher will play an increasingly important role along with the SLP and parent. The best chances of a child with SLI or LLD growing into a functional and independent individual is when such specialised intervention is provided over several years with integrated input from all concerned.

Early and intensive language treatment with parent involvement in language stimulation is the best course of action for the child with SLI. The younger the child, the more likely that there will be spontaneous improvement. Since the signs of SLI are evident by the age of three years the child should be provided with an enriched language environment. The SLP can train the parents to provide intensive speech stimulation to their offspring and also in techniques that elicit speech from children. Such home training can be coupled with enrolment in preschool programs that enhance vocabulary building and interaction between children, with intensive language stimulation. The other normally developing children often serve as role models.

Children with SLI need to be provided with additional opportunities to talk and to listen. Paradoxically, a child with language impairment ends up receiving even fewer opportunities than his normally developing peer, because those in his environment do not have the patience or because communication with him is not as rewarding to the adult as it is with his other peers. The likelihood of peer interaction for a child with SLI is even less because a child his age will not be capable of making up for his deficits as an older child or adult will. Thus the nature of the disability itself limits the child's exposure to adequate language stimulation, which is in fact what he needs most. Language therapy targets the child's ability to understand language, learn new words, learn the rules of language and generally help the child to develop language that is appropriate for his age. It is important to talk to these children for like all children, they model their language behaviour after the adults in their environment. Learning to listen is important for language acquisition. Get them to listen to the different sounds in their environment and to the speech that surrounds them. Get them to listen to what you say and how you say it. Encourage tasks that emphasise narratives and the sharing of information. Learning to express thoughts and feelings through language is important and should be supported. Talk to the child about a variety of experiences. Supplement this by reading to him. As the child grows older, encourage him to read independently but follow this up with a discussion of what is read. Integrate language support with academics. Speech-language therapy may need to be continued throughout the school years either in one on one sessions or through a consultant-monitoring basis.

School Support

The management of children with SLI in India involves the added dimension of multilingualism. Children in India are invariably exposed to more than one language and often have to study a minimum of three languages over the school years. In most instances, at least in urban India, English remains the first choice for the medium of instruction, with the national and state or foreign language as second and third languages. It is advisable to provide the child with language impairment, education in his mother tongue in order to prevent him from being overburdened in an area that is already of concern, by expecting him to seek education in a medium which he is not familiar with and has difficulty learning in. In addition there is some evidence to indicate that the acquisition of languages in which the grammatical morphemes often provide a distinct ending or sound for each new tense, and verbs are inflected for tense and grammatical agreement as in Italian and Spanish, were not nearly as difficult as compared to English. Most Indian languages are agglutinative in nature with inflected morphemes and it follows that they too should be relatively easier for the child with SLI to learn. When compounded with the fact that the Indian language is often the mother tongue and therefore would be the strongest language of the child, it provides us with formidable reasons for educating children with language impairments in their mother tongue. Exemption from having to learn more than one language at school for children with learning disabilities is being provided in a few Indian states as of now. It is important that these provisions are extended to all children with developmental language disorders, including those with SLI, across the country.

Parental Support

The identification of the problem in SLI is a difficult process given the near total lack of awareness of such a condition among the professionals and the public, in our country. Parents, therefore, should play a proactive role in identification, since early identification leads to early intervention and its long term benefits. It also leads to reassurance, particularly of the child with SLI who often resorts to temper tantrums and aggressive behaviour because of the frustration arising out of his inability to communicate adequately. Parents should make efforts to understand the child if necessary by providing alternates, but at the same time deal with the tantrums firmly and consistently and not accept tantrums as a mode of communication. The emphasis in communication should be on what the child wants to say rather than how s/he says it. Similar help may need to be provided in his interactions and play with peers. Apart from providing reassurance, building a supportive language environment in the home, with a greater focus on sharing experiences and feelings verbally rather than emphasising academic skills such as reciting the alphabet, is needed for the child with SLI. Reading to the child with simplified text, a lot of visuals and contextual clues is also recommended.

Fullsome praise for the things that s/he is good at, will go a long way in building self esteem.

6

Semantic Pragmatic Deficits or Pragmatic Language Impairments

The 1970s and 80s witnessed a focus on the study of the acquisition of linguistic communication by children. During this period there was a spate of studies on the acquisition of specific linguistic aspects of language such as the acquisition of phonology, syntax and semantics. By the 1980s and 90s the focus had shifted to the acquisition of language within a broader framework of the use of language in a context. Unlike the linguistic perspective of language, which is one of a formal and context independent system, this perspective, which came to be known as the pragmatic viewpoint emphasised the importance of the rules that govern the use of language in a functional contextual model.

With the increasing array of tools that evolved for the assessment of different aspects of language in children, from the 1970s onwards, the description and the identification of the subtypes of language acquisition disorders also became more sophisticated. One of these newly identified types of developmental language disorders is the 'semantic-pragmatic disorder' (SPD) or 'semantic-pragmatic language disorder (SPLD). As the name implies these children characteristically have deficits in the semantic and pragmatic aspects of language. However, as the data on semantic-pragmatic disorders built up over the last decade or so, it became increasingly clear that the deficit primarily affects pragmatics rather than semantics and pragmatics, and is possibly linked to 'social cognition'. Hence the term 'pragmatic language impairment' (PLI) is now being used more frequently instead of the older term 'semantic-pragmatic disorder'. At times the two are used interchangeably.

There is also now an increased focus on the acquisition of the advanced language skills by adolescents in the age range of 13–18 years. They consist of increasingly precise use of the lexicon, use of figurative language such as idioms and puns and peer group slang, the increasing use of complex passive and embedded sentences, the ability to grasp overall meanings of narratives without getting distracted by the details and conversely mastering good narrative skills such as in story telling with adequate connectiveness and cohesion. Good conversational skills with the ability to choose the correct register in social conversations are also increasingly mastered during these years. The adolescent with a communication impairment affecting these aspects of language, is likely to have considerable difficulty in establishing stable peer relationships, leading to maladjustments in other areas of social and psychological development. Unlike the developmental language disorders that are seen in preschool years, these difficulties in advanced language acquisition are less obvious and more difficult to identify and are often referred to as an 'invisible disability'. Nevertheless, since they have an impact on the academic performance and the social skills of the adolescent, they are referred to by terms such as 'school-related difficulty' or 'difficulty socialising'. These deficits in 'higher language acquisition' will be described in this chapter and discussed again in the next chapter on 'learning disabilities', given their symbiotic relationship with the learning disabilities.

Definition

Semantics is the aspect of language function that relates to the acquisition of words, their meanings and their use in speech, both in isolation and as a part of phrases and sentences. It also covers the interrelatedness of words and the different ways in which words relate to each other. Pragmatics is that aspect of language that covers aspects of the use of language in social context. It refers to the use of language as well as the broader communication skills that are needed to interact appropriately with others in different social situations. It includes both verbal and nonverbal aspects of language in a social interactional context and the awareness and application of a set of rules that dictate our body posture, proximity and eye contact when interacting with others, 'knowing what to say, how to say and when to say it, and also conversational skills such as introducing a topic, taking turns at the conversation, maintaining a topic or signalling a change in topic and ending a conversation.

As assessments of children with language disorders became more detailed, it became clear that there was a subgroup of children with developmental language disorders in whom language for everyday purposes was present, but who seemed to have a specific difficulty in conveying their meaning in social conversational situations. Despite their fluent speech with good articulation these children had difficulty comprehending verbal inputs such as instructions. Their verbal output was characterised by lack of precision and they had specific difficulty in taking turns and maintaining a conversation. The terms semantic-pragmatic syndrome' (SPS) or 'semantic-pragmatic disorder' (SPD) or 'semantic-pragmatic language disorder' (SPLD) were introduced to label this particular subgroup of developmental language disorders in the 1980s. Since the turn of the century, however, the term 'pragmatic language impairment' is being used more widely to refer to the same subgroup since it is increasingly becoming clear that the deficit lies primarily in pragmatics or the social use of language, the deficits in semantics being a byproduct of the primary disorder at the pragmatic level.

In addition to the pragmatic disorders, which are commonly identified in late childhood or the primary school years, there is an awareness that even those children who have gone on to high school without any 'language problem' being identified in them, may come up with a language problem when faced with the complexities of language at high school. These 'language disorders' overlap with the 'learning disabilities' but they are not the same.

While some children with learning disabilities have language disorders, the two can exist separately. That is, there are some children who have reading and writing difficulties with no language disorders, while others have language disorders with no reading and writing difficulties. However in the latter, as the academic level goes higher, the language disorder is bound to impact the individual's reading and writing performance too. As indicated earlier, our concern here is with the group of children whose language disorder surfaces in high school and who have no specific learning disabilities. The language disorders that are more directly associated with learning disability will be dealt with in the next chapter on "Learning Disability".

Incidence and Prevalence

Incidence figures for the existence of SPD or PLI are difficult to come by; particularly since there are an increasing number of researchers who are voicing the opinion that children diagnosed with SPD or PLI are in fact part of the larger spectrum of pervasive developmental disorders or the autistic spectrum disorders, rather than having a pure language disorder. This argument is supported by observations that even when the language of these children improves they still have considerable social difficulties. Hence, while the term continues to be used as a descriptive term, it is not being used as a diagnostic label, since it does not take into consideration the underlying socio-cognitive deficits. We will return to this issue in chapter 11 on autistic spectrum disorders.

Literature on the higher order language skills and their mastery by children has largely been compiled in the latter half of the twentieth century. It is now acknowledged that a substantial number of adolescents have difficulty mastering these subtle and gradually acquired communication skills, leading to considerable academic failure and school dropout. However, the prevalence rates of children with deficits in these areas is not known, since there has been relatively less research in this area. About three to five percent of high school students are estimated to have learning disabilities and about the same proportion probably have language disorders. Most of them are boys.

Characteristics

Research literature on the acquisition of words and word meanings by children, which is the acquisition of semantics, is quite extensive and much debated. Beginning with first words around the age of one year, by six years children are reported to have a vocabulary of about 4,000 to 5,000 word families going up to 20,000 by young adulthood and expanding gradually after that, depending on individual circumstances. It is generally believed that children acquire words by identifying words in the speech stream and guessing at their meaning, when heard repeatedly in given contexts. In the process, they sometimes 'over generalise', that is extend the meaning of a word to others which share their attributes, for e.g. calling a 'goat ' a 'dog' and under extension, that is failing to include a word with given attributes to its class, as for e. g in failing to identify a Pekinese as a 'dog'. Through this trial and error process, children not only acquire a large vocabulary within a span of few years but also become sensitive to the relationships between words for e.g. 'big' and 'small' (antonym), 'fat' and 'stout' (synonym) and so on.

Pragmatic skills start developing early in life. Though the early turn-taking exchanges between mother and infant may be more nonverbal than verbal-they lay the foundation for later verbal exchanges and the development of pragmatic skills. More complex aspects of pragmatic skills are acquired through infancy and the early school years culminating in the most complex use of pragmatic skills, as seen in conversational skills and social use of language in adolescence and adulthood.

Disorders

Children with semantic-pragmatic disorders are very likely to be described as having been quiet babies who did not communicate or interact much with limited babbling, reduced and poor response to speech stimuli, not much pointing or sharing and were possibly late in acquiring speech. They may have a disproportionate number of nouns in their early vocabulary and may be slow in acquiring verbs. Children who have semantic deficits have difficulties in understanding the meaning of words as well as in acquiring words, and in rapidly retrieving the words they know. They have particular trouble with abstract words and words that relate to emotions and feelings. They tend to interpret all speech literally and have great difficulty in understanding word play, idioms, puns and slang. They also have difficulty in grasping the key points of messages and discourse and tend to be overly influenced by any one word or two in the interpretation of sentences.

Children with pragmatic deficits on the other hand are characteristically poor conversationalists. They tend not to bother about social greetings and have difficulty in initiating and carrying on a social conversation. They are seldom interested in, or able to follow conversational topics that do not relate to them directly and often talk non-stop about their own interests. They have difficulty in monitoring their intonations and use either a flat or exaggerated intonation pattern. As a result their conversation can sound too grown up or rude. They also have difficulty in choosing the correct register for their conversational partners, that is when and whom to address formally or informally, and are noted for their use of tactless expressions. They fail to judge and take into consideration the prior knowledge of their conversational partner and either talk down to them or else make no sense to them. The have difficulties in introducing, maintaining and ending topics in conversations. They tend to learn language by memorising and will tend to focus on specifics in conversation while missing out on the general meaning. As a result they will appear immature in their conversations. Pragmatic skills also include being tuned to the body language of the conversational partner, maintaining adequate eye contact and knowing when to take one's turn. As a result of not paying adequate attention to these nonverbal cues, their communicative behaviour appears either irrelevant or rude and inconsiderate and they end up losing the interest of the listener.

Children with SPD/PLI have a host of difficulties in both the receptive and expressive aspects of language. They show specific comprehension deficits particularly in response to questions, which are not in synchrony with their fluent and well-articulated speech. They tend to get carried away by a word or two in a sentence, without waiting to grasp the meaning of the sentence as a whole. They often exhibit poor listening skills resulting in difficulties in tasks that require precision, such as following directions and grasping the essence of a lecture or narrative. They perform better with concrete step by step instructions and are particularly poor in understanding slang or jargon, making them misfits in adolescent social banter, which are particularly rich in these aspects. When speaking, they have difficulties in word retrieval, and lack precision in word use, resulting in broken sentences with false starts, circumlocutory speech or beating around the bush with frequent use of empty phrases. Their understanding of the relations between words and the multiple meanings that a word can have is inadequate. They are unable to give clear directions or explain specific concepts and confuse their listeners. Their conversations are characterised by abruptness and abrasiveness as they consistently violate conversational rules. These communicative difficulties are also manifested in their reading and writing skills affecting their ability to process information through the written mode and consequently their thinking and reasoning skills too. The broad based nature of the deficit is also evident in their nonverbal communication since they often have difficulty in interpreting facial expressions. They misinterpret the body movements of others and themselves have awkward movements. They misjudge and often violate social rules for physical proximity that are culturally determined. As a result children with pragmatic difficulties have great trouble using language socially, in ways that are appropriate for their age. This in turn leads to embarrassment and frustration in the child who may be faced with both criticism and mocking. For instance, they may have difficulty in understanding jokes and following conversations, resulting in exclusion from peer groups. One of their greatest difficulties lies in forming friendships. They may alternately be seen as naïve and childish or as domineering and a bully. It is therefore important to understand the nature of this disorder and handle it appropriately both at home and school. SPD or PLI is a complex disorder that is not yet fully understood.

At the high school level children are required to master even more complex verbal skills to accommodate increasingly complex academic demands. In some children the 'language disorder' may surface only at this level. Their speech may be less effortless than that of their peers. They may be unable to follow long stories or narrations and similar difficulties may be seen in their written output. The language disorder in these individuals may not be apparent and their oral language skills are seldom examined, since they have developed early language reasonably well. Their difficulties often become evident only when faced with the higher-level demands of high school. On evaluation they often come up with verbal intelligence quotient (IQ) scores that are significantly lower than performance IQ scores. Since classroom interactions are highly dependent on verbal interactions the student will fail to perform adequately in this demanding verbal environment. The consequences of such unidentified language disorders could also be perceived as attention disorders or behaviour disorders.

Children who have subtle language disorders that manifest at the high school level often have a cluster of symptoms. They may be reluctant speakers, but when they do speak they may sound garrulous with empty speech full of clichés and overuse of some words and phrases with lots of fillers such 'umm' and 'uh uh' and empty words such as 'this' and 'that'. They have difficulty in using complex grammar and cannot logically explain issues. They have difficulty with abstract language and ideas and take a long time to process such information. They also tend to have difficulties with schoolwork such as homework, non-participation in classroom activities, inability to follow class schedules and routines, giving and gathering information and working independently. Their attention and concentration, as also their performance in tests are poor. In addition they have poor play skills, poor self-esteem, loss of motivation, difficulties in making and maintaining friendships and may show depression, anger, frustration and aggression. While these problems can result from causes other than language problems, the point is that language problems are seldom looked for and ruled out in these cases, whereas in fact they might be the root cause of some of these behavioural and school problems.

Causes

The causes of these higher order developmental language disorders (DLD) are not as yet clearly established. However a strong case for a genetic basis is being made, given that these subtle language disorders seem to run in families, that is, the chances of other family members having a similar problem is higher among the families of those identified as having a developmental language disorder, as compared to their typically developing peers. DLD is also more common among monozygotic twins. Developmental language disorders such as pragmatic language impairment are also seen as a part of the continuum of pervasive developmental disorders such as autistic spectrum disorders.

Referral and Assessment

Higher order language disorders in children are only now being widely recognised. As such it is the formally trained speech-language pathologist that is likely to be most familiar with these conditions and should be the professional referred to first. Formal language assessments by SLPs target an assessment of the child's mastery of each of the aspects involved—semantics, pragmatics and discourse, as compared with their peers or established norms. While a marked difference between a student's verbal and nonverbal abilities is a hallmark of a language disorder, it must also be remembered that with these subtle language disorders, the performance on a one on one language test may be good, with the everyday language performance in real life situation at odds with the performance in a controlled test situation. Assessment and intervention efforts may, therefore, be focused on the playground or the home rather than on academic or clinical test situations per se. Assessments are also carried out to establish whether the language disorder is present in isolation or along with any other speech disorder such as a verbal dyspraxia or an articulation disorder. Co-occurring disorders such as cognitive and behavioural disorders too have to be assessed and ruled out. The possibility of the language disorder suggesting a diagnostic possibility such as Autistic Spectrum Disorders (ASD) or Asperger's has to be looked into and involves other specialists such as developmental paediatricians, neurophysicians and psychologists.

Intervention

Clinical intervention for the child with SPD, like that for other children with communication disorders have to be geared to the particular needs of a given child within an enriched language environment. Children with SPD/PLI are known to have some difficulties in auditory verbal comprehension such as difficulties in listening in noisy environments or in following specific verbal instructions. It is therefore necessary to enhance their listening skills and verbal comprehension. Reduction of the linguistic complexity of speech addressed to them often helps them to comprehend better. However the focus here is on the child's use of language rather than specific linguistic aspects such as the correction of the speech sounds or grammar. It is the use of language for a variety of functions such as greeting, questioning, commenting, requesting, affirming, negating, et cetera that needs to be taught, taking advantage of naturally occurring interactions. New words have to be introduced in a careful, explicit manner with ample opportunities provided to the child for mastering them in a conceptually ordered, hierarchical fashion. Language scaffolding will help in extension of the child's use of his newly acquired vocabulary. Role-play may also be used to model appropriate communication behaviour in different set-ups with different people. Once the child masters specific roles, it is advisable to provide role reversal opportunities so as to facilitate his participation in conversations both as a speaker and a listener.

The child needs to be aware of the fact that speech has a range of functions from social pleasantries such as greeting and polite enquiries to commenting, requesting, affirming, negating, and so on. The different aspects of a conversational exchange such as a topic, the need to take turns in conversations and selecting a style that is appropriate to the conversational partner, needs to be emphasised. The importance of developing effective persuasion, and good conversational and narrative skills, has to be emphasised and demonstrated through examples. It is also important to illustrate that conversations can break down when these norms are not followed and how to repair such a breakdown by requesting a repetition or clarification and by rephrasing and revising one's own speech. The supportive role of nonverbal signals such as a facial expression or body posture, for a smooth conversation has to be shown. This will further instil the necessary confidence in social communication. Idioms and similes pose a special problem for children with SPD and need to be avoided or clearly explained in concrete language. Children with SPD/PLI often respond much better to visual cues and it is therefore recommended that visual props such as drawings and written instructions are used widely.

Group support should be provided to increase their sociability and monitor their progress in a variety of play situations to extend their play skills to play with peers and pretend play. These activities will help in developing an understanding of other people's mind, which is an essential ingredient of good conversation and social communication. Skills in inferring and predicting the behaviour of others should then be worked on. Some children with SPD may have extraordinary memory skills, particularly for specific skills such as maps and routes. Some have an excellent memory for printed words and signs and others for tunes. These special skills need to be supported and used to build the child's self esteem.

School Support

In the classroom, however, the SPD child's performance is often patchy, with him excelling in a few areas and performing well below par on others. Some children with SPD learn to associate printed words with meaning directly even before formally being taught to read – a phenomenon termed 'hyperlexia'. However, not all of this translates into reading and comprehending text. Others find reading and writing difficult and are often diagnosed with dyslexia as well. A distinct difference is often observed in the practical application of skills that are present. For instance, while a given child may be good at mathematics his ability to apply it in a social transaction such as shopping may be well below that expected by his mathematical skills. These need to be addressed by concrete examples and actual practice under monitored conditions.

Writing and creative writing may also be areas of concern. Handwriting may often remain illegible despite years of training and it might be better to train the child on a word processor. Creative writing like pretend play is a grey area and needs extra attention and practice.

Most children with SPD/PLI in India are likely to be enrolled in the regular classroom without an acknowledgement of their condition or any specific support being provided to them. It is likely that several of them may end up as school dropouts and some enrolled in special schools. Given that many of these are brighter than average and can perform very well in mainstream schools, it is crucial to identify their difficulties and assist them by providing them with specialised professional support such as speech-language therapy as well as additional support in school, with good coordination between the two. Change in classroom routines should be planned and explained to a child with PLI to facilitate his adjustments to these changes. Being specifically told what is acceptable and what is not, in class and setting the rules clearly will go a long way in dealing with the behavioural issues that may be consequent to the core communication and social difficulty. Finally, there is the issue of teasing and bullying that is common in classrooms. Frequently children with communication disorders such as SPD/PLI will gain some insight in to the fact that they are in some ways functioning differently than their peers. It is important to help the child deal with this insight, accept it and work around it. It is also important for the teacher to explain to other children why it is that the child with this disorder cannot conform like others in the class and to ensure that he is not subjected to undue peer pressure both inside and outside of the classroom.

In brief, the child with PLI needs to be supported in social understanding and its impact on his environment. They need to be trained specifically in social skills and pragmatics and provided with the motivation to communicate. Assistance should be provided to enhance attending and listening skills as well as play skills. Language therapy should be directed towards enhancement of both receptive and expressive language and may be achieved through structured but non-directive communication therapy programmes. The use of visual cues, social stories, and role-play are often particularly beneficial. All key individuals, such as the therapist, teacher and family need to be involved in the process.

Language disorders in adolescence have the dual effects of both interfering and impacting the child's academic performance as well as his social and eventual personal self-realisation. The wider social implications of the effects of such a language disorder in terms of valuable human resources need to be understood fully in order to appreciate the need for effective intervention. Subtle language disorders in high school students can easily be missed. When in doubt, it is best to have an appropriate assessment and intervention from a SLP. However, the classroom teacher also has a vital role to play in this area. The first step is to consider the possibility that a language disorder may underlie the problems faced by the child and to take steps towards clarifying this position.

Classroom teachers can play an important role in identifying and aiding an adolescent with an 'invisible language disorder'. These children are likely to be disruptive in class and in need of additional educational support. The teacher is ideally placed to support and aid language intervention for these children as the necessary activities can be blended into regular classroom activities and will also enable the child to actively use and generalise his new found skills, as he masters them. As a rule teachers probe and support the reading and writing skills of such children. However it is important to be aware that the child may have oral language difficulties, which may be more pervasive and in fact underlie the written language difficulties.

Discussions on the specifics of an article or story that has been read, outlining stories and narrations around a central theme, compiling lists of significant facts, details or information, and ordering them according to headings, linking cause and effect, drawing the moral of a story, identifying unfamiliar words and discussing their possible meanings, generating ideas about stories based on their title are some of the tasks that can be employed to help an adolescent with an invisible language disorder in the classroom. Feedback on classroom activities from students, modifying speed and content of presentations based on such feedback, encouraging and rewarding students' seeking clarifications and help, can go a long way in assisting the child with a language disorder to participate more fully in the classroom.

Careful control over the amount of new vocabulary that is presented, the extensive use of audiovisual supports in the classroom, speech supported by gestures and actions, and illustrations, will aid comprehension. A variety of strategies to aid memory can also be introduced. Above all, it is important for the teacher to monitor his or her own speech and make it as direct as possible, with explanations and restatements provided when metaphorical language is used. Instructions need to be explicit and supported by clear written instructions that are graded in small steps. Effective study skills such as note-taking, time management, organisational systems, and the use of communication books between school and home need to be explicitly taught. Peer acceptance and peer interaction also needs to be aided, given their specific social difficulties. It is also important for the teacher to understand that behavioural issues such as non-compliance and inattention may in fact be maladaptations to the communication difficulties and to accept them as such. Finally, it is important to regularly interact with the others who are concerned with the child's communication difficulties such as his parents, as well as SLP, special educator and counsellor, when available.

Teachers and SLPs should combine their expertise in working with children who have communication disorders, wherever possible. This is not the monopoly of the therapist or the teacher. Joint assessment and goal setting with implementation shared between the two in a manner that is suited to the individual being trained and the interactional set up with the child would be the quickest and most effective strategy. Teachers play a crucial role when the child with a communication disorder is transiting between the different stages of school as well as when he is ready to leave school. The need for explicit training in formal communication skills is increasingly being emphasised in modern society and there is increasing awareness that these may need to be introduced within the school.

Over the last couple of decades, the role of metalinguistic skills in a child's mastery of language for academic purposes has drawn considerable attention. This phenomenon will be presented and discussed in the following chapter in the context of language and learning disabilities.

Parental Support

Pragmatic skills are used across a variety of situations and are particularly important in social situations. It is therefore vital that there is good collaboration between the therapists, teachers and parents in the management of pragmatic skill training. The ultimate test of pragmatic skills training is the ease with which the child communicates appropriately and effectively across social situations. This can only be achieved and monitored with regular interaction between all three at every stage - that is identification, evaluation, training and generalisation; of the child with pragmatic and other higher order language disorders, on the lines suggested above.

7

Learning Disabilities

The term 'learning disability' has now become familiar to us as being indicative of a condition in which children have a range of learning difficulties in school. When learning disability (LD) was first identified and described in the nineteenth century, in the early work of physicians like Orton, it was in fact focused on reading difficulties. Orton described specific difficulties in learning to read in otherwise typically growing children. He, however, did mention that these children often had spoken language deficits. As the learning disabilities movement acquired momentum in the mid-twentieth century, the focus shifted from reading and language to a broader perspective including more basic visuomotor and auditory processing difficulties that interfered in academic learning in otherwise normal children. More recently, the observation that children with learning difficulties seldom overcame their difficulties on a sustained basis, despite early intervention on visuomotor and auditory processing including training in phonic skills, coupled with the increasing sensitivity to the language acquisition process that emerged in the latter half of the twentieth century, made it clear that language learning difficulties underlie a considerable portion of the learning difficulties of a child with LD. Consequently the focus has once again shifted to language disability so much so that the term 'language learning disability' is now, at times, used interchangeably with the term 'learning disability'.

Definition

The most common description of 'Learning Disability' is that it is a difficulty in learning that is not due to any specific cause such as a sensory or motor impairment, or mental retardation or due to lack of adequate exposure to schooling. These children show a marked discrepancy between their potential and their academic performance and this discrepancy cannot be accounted for by any other known factor including educational and socio-economic opportunity. They have no specific sensory motor deficits, their overall functioning in all developmental domains falls within the normal range and they have had adequate exposure to and training in literacy skills.

Since the 1980s the broad definition of LD formulated by the U.S. National Joint Committee on LD with representation from all concerned disciplines, has been widely used and is reproduced here: LD is a general term that refers to a heterogeneous group of disorders manifested by significant difficulties in the acquisition and use of listening, speaking, reading, writing, reasoning or mathematical abilities. These disorders are intrinsic to the individual, presumed to be due to central nervous system dysfunction and may occur across the lifespan. Problems in self-regulatory behaviours, social perception and social interaction may exist with learning disabilities but do not by themselves constitute a learning disability. Although learning disabilities may occur concomitantly with other handicapping conditions (for example sensory impairment, mental retardation, serious emotional disturbance) or with extrinsic influences such as cultural differences, insufficient or inappropriate instruction, they are not the result of these conditions or influences.

Most definitions of LD remain vague and identify themselves by way of negative markers or by ruling out other specified causes that could lead to difficulties in learning, rather than by positively identifying specific causes or factors that result in learning disability. Much of the earlier work on LD and its definition have focused on children in their early school years. In recent years however, there is an increasing awareness that there is a wide array of learning disorders, which interfere with the academic progress of adolescents. These learning disorders are only now beginning to be recognised and documented and as yet there is no satisfactory terminology or definitions that encompass them.

As the student moves from the primary to high school, there is a gradual shift in teaching style from student-oriented, oral classroom teaching to increasingly content-oriented teaching that draws heavily from written material. The style of narrative text changes from direct to the indirect or implied. The linguistic and communication skills that an individual is required to learn through the adolescent years are subtle and difficulties in the same are more difficult to identify. These subtle language deficits place enormous demands on the child's attentional capacity and interfere with the comprehension and thinking process. Deficits in these advanced skills of language also result in problems in reading and writing as well as in critical, logical and scientific reasoning, all of which are essential for academic success during and beyond the school years. Eventually these difficulties tend to establish a vicious cycle of failure, in which the learning disabled child gets poorer in achievement, motivation, confidence, self-esteem, social relationships and attitudes to school.

With the increasing sensitivity and growing awareness of the unsuitability of traditional classroom teaching techniques to the particular strengths and interests of the learning disabled adolescent, it is likely that the traditional criteria and definitions of learning disability will be rephrased in the coming years to reflect its complexity.

Incidence and Prevalence

Given the lack of agreement about the definition of LD, figures on the incidence and prevalence of LD can vary widely. Estimates vary from 4 to 10 per cent of school children. In India, well-controlled large-scale studies are hard to come by. In the last decade an extensive study carried out in Kerala, which employed a broad definition of LD, suggested that nearly 10 per cent of children and adolescents up to the age of 18 years, were found to have learning difficulties.

Characteristics

The most common characteristic of a child with a learning disability is an unaccounted failure in learning to read. On closer observation it is often seen that these children are poor in auditory processing, as seen in their difficulties in learning rhymes, poor speech discrimination, and problems in following directions and word games. They also have poor short term or immediate memory for verbal materials and have a marked difficulty in retrieving words from memory. They may remember details in stories but have difficulty in constructing the gist or summarising. Often there is a history of delay or deficits in oral language or speech, such as an articulation or a fluency disorder. As mentioned in Chapter 5 children diagnosed as having specific language impairment at an early age often face difficulties in literacy acquisition in school. At school there are significant difficulties in spelling and mastering writing. Some Western studies report that the prevalence of specific reading difficulties among children with a history of preschool language impairment increases from 6 per cent to 24 per cent between the ages of 8 and 15 years.

Other than these language related deficits, children with LD may also exhibit other characteristics such as poor auditory-visual integration, visual functioning, perceptual-motor skills, hand-eye coordination, automatising skills, and arithmetic. In addition to, or perhaps consequent to these difficulties they may show poor motivation. They often appear disorganised and have poor social skills with low self-esteem. At times co-morbid behavioural disorders such as conduct disorder or oppositional defiant disorder and depression may also be present.

Disorders

Learning disabilities have been categorised into subtypes by several researchers. The most common classification is that of disorders of reading, disorders of writing and disorders of mathematics. Others classify them as dyslexia (specific reading disability), nonverbal learning disabilities and language learning disabilities. Often, a given child may have more than one type of LD.

In the recent past there has been a substantial broadening of the concept of learning disorder to include older children who lack many of the higher-order thinking skills required of self-directed learning, which is the eventual goal of all education. The difficulties of these children may appear to be less severe but they often lead to a multitude of academic, social and behavioural problems leading to high dropout rates.

Difficulties in writing are also frequently associated with learning disabilities. They may be of two basic types – the first due to a graphomotor difficulty and the second due to higher order deficits. In the first, written output may be illegible. These children often have poor fine motor coordination of the fingers. The second type of writing difficulties reflect the difficulties that these children have with language, organisational problems and other higher order deficits such as in problem solving, planning and revising strategies to make a text cohesive and coherent. It must also be remembered that during the developmental process all these cognitive processes are interdependent and can influence each other. A deficit in one will necessarily have an effect on the others.

Causes

The specific aetiology of LD is still unknown. However there is growing evidence that it is possibly neurological and could have a genetic basis. There is now a considerable body of literature that the incidence of learning disabilities is higher in families and identical twins. There is genetic evidence that children born in to families of individuals with reading disabilities are likely to have a 50 per cent chance of becoming reading disabled.

LDs are also assumed to result from deficits in information processing. Subtle sensory deficits in visual and auditory processing have also been cited among the causative factors linked to LD. While they are not visually or auditorily impaired, they are observed to have difficulty in processing rapidly produced auditory stimuli, termed as auditory processing disorder, or in visually scanning printed material, a phenomenon known as visual persistence in which the readers experience blurred vision for letters and letters that move around. Processing speed, in particular, has been singled out as a causative factor for LD as these children appear to have difficulty in processing information that is presented rapidly, not only in terms of comprehending language but also in retrieving words and in other non language tasks such as pressing a button in choosing between a high and low tone. The presence of other motor difficulties such as the apraxias and difficulties in motor balance have led to a hypothesis that they have problems in mastering any skill that should become automatic with practice and are said to be suggestive of a cerebellar deficit.

Referral and Assessments

Since most definitions of LD lack specificity the most commonly used approach to the identification of LD is what is referred to as thc discrepancy formula. According to this formula, everything else being normal, if a child does not acquire reading skills after two years of sustained teaching or falls behind his peers from similar backgrounds by about 2 years then s/he could be suspected to have a learning disability. This of course necessitates that the child is enrolled in school for at least two years, before an identification of LD can be made.

However there are others who argue that children 'at risk' can be efficiently identified earlier in pre school. Such identification, they argue, can be made on the basis of a neurodevelopmental perspective, since the educational perspective that is commonly associated with LD cannot be applied to them; on the basis of precursors of academic skills specifically oral expression, listening comprehension, pre-writing, pre-reading and pre-mathematic skills, as also attention, memory, perceptual and motor skills, thinking and nonverbal abilities. LD in preschool years may be expressed as deficits in uses of language, speech and reasoning and may co occur with problems in social interactions and in motor skills or regulation. These children have abilities and behaviours that are different or discrepant from normative expectancies and these are not explainable by sensory limitations, general cognitive deficits or disadvantaged environments.

Neurodevelopmental indicators are used to identify preschoolers at risk for subsequent learning disabilities. Neurological soft signs including gross and fine motor coordination problems, abnormal movements, reflex asymmetries and visual motor abnormality are often present. Some standard tests for identification of LD in preschool children have been developed with components on visual perceptual, motor and language skills. Checklists that are based largely on language factors such as phonological awareness are also increasingly used for this purpose. Poor attention and concentration in preschoolers have been identified as high indicators of children at risk for LD. Those who advocate early identification of LD recommend it in order to reduce and prevent frustration building in the child and to prevent the cascade effect. However, others feel that given the lack of a sound theoretical basis it may become a self-fulfilling prophecy.

Despite the enormous interest in the early identification of learning disabilities, there is as yet no single reliable method of predicting it. Potential risk factors such as distractibility, poor attention, difficulties in the acquisition of alphabetic knowledge and phonological factors such as poor phonological awareness, short-term memory and retrieval are often cited as risk factors. Perceptual difficulties in processing rapidly presented verbal material and family history of others with reading difficulties would further substantiate the case for checking out LD. However there is no general agreement about how one could routinely identify a child in school as being learning disabled. Experienced teachers can generally identify a child with learning disability by comparing his overall capabilities with his difficulties in the academic set-up relative to his peers. Some formal tools for screening school children and identifying those with potential LD have recently been developed.

It is important that when a teacher suspects a child of possibly having a learning disability, a referral is made to a specialist in the area, for a complete assessment, help in developing a suitable intervention plan and management of co morbid disorders if any. This could be a psychologist, an SLP or a physician who specialises in developmental disorders. A complete language assessment by an SLP would involve a profile on speech, language, reading and writing tests including checking out auditory skills, phonological awareness, oro-motor abilities, reading comprehension, verbal expression and spelling.

Such a profile will lead to an identification of the affected modality and level of difficulty, its impact on learning and the coping strategies used by the child, which would in turn form the basis for remediation.

Several tools for the assessment of learning difficulties have been developed in the West and are commercially available. Apart from being expensive these are not culturally and linguistically suitable for even the English speaking children in our country, as they have been developed and standardised for Western children whose primary language is English, and within a Western cultural context. Some attempts to develop indigenous tools both in English and Indian languages have been made and a few of these are cited in the books listed at the end of this book.

Current western tests for reading disability focus substantially on phonological skills and awareness, given the close relation that has been hypothesised between reading and phonological awareness in alphabetic writing systems like English. In general, however, tests for identification and assessment for learning disability include components on listening skills, grapheme-phoneme correspondences and word decoding. It is important to rule out broader language deficits before arriving at a conclusion of reading disability.

Intervention

Specifics of intervention for LD would depend on the age at which a child is identified and the presenting signs of LD. In this chapter we will be focusing on the aspects of language support that a child with LD might require. This too would be dependent on the age and stage of language acquisition that a given child is in, at a given time. For instance, at the preschool level, phonological impairments, difficulties in rapid naming and naming of letters may be the most obvious difficulty. In primary school, grammatical difficulties and lack of fluency in communication may interfere with learning the most, and in higher grades it might be slow and poor comprehension of both verbal and written material. As the complexity of the academic demands in higher grades increase, spelling and writing difficulties may appear more prominently.

Current interventions for language based learning disabilities generally target the phonological processing skills in preschoolers and early schoolers, and language comprehension in older children. Phonological awareness training focuses on explicit letter knowledge and various types of manipulations of the phonemes in a word so as to sensitise the child to the mapping of the letter sound to the letter, leading to better reading. The other focus of training addresses verbal comprehension and is generally used with older children. They address skills related to semantic memory and retrieval, using context to facilitate comprehension, story and text recall, summarising what is read and self-correction. Organisational cues and cueing strategies are also emphasised in order to facilitate reading comprehension. It is incorrect to presume that these older children will simply outgrow their problems. They need language intervention to help learn new vocabulary, organise their thoughts and use language appropriately in a variety of contexts. This includes training in how to be a good listener and a good narrator. Several programmes for older children with learning disabilities provide interventions that are both language-based and academic skill-based and improve overall communication skills.

School Support

Along with professional intervention, children with LD require specialised attention at school with adequate support and encouragement at home. To be able to provide such attention the teacher needs to be aware of fine-grained recognition of the variety of learning disabilities. Such awareness on the part of the teacher is also required to implement specific interventions that target specific learning problems. The teacher is ideally placed to observe and document the error patterns and behaviour, as also the learning strengths of a given child, which will supplement the information derived from formal testing, in providing a direction for designing and monitoring the intervention programme. Such overall assistance from the classroom teacher can go a long way in the development and successful implementation of intervention programmes for children with LD.

Some of the specific areas of concern in the classroom management of adolescents with learning disability are poor attention, poor memory, inadequate or superficial comprehension of verbal instructions and immature verbal expression. In the early school years classroom speech games, which target phonological skills with concrete manipulatives and visualisations along with mnemonic devices and extensive practice, are highly useful. As the child moves on to higher grades, enhancement of speed and comprehension in reading can be targeted, by expanding his vocabulary and speed practice with repeated readings. Assistive technology such as the use of computerised text readers and note takers can also be employed. Even later, in middle and high school, teachers will need to use highly explicit instruction, which aims at developing all components of reading and writing. For this the teacher would need a strong knowledge base in language and all aspects of reading. Choice of a particular aspect and the sequence in which intervention needs to be provided will be determined by a given child's functional level. Students may then be paired or placed in small homogenous groups for activities that involve directed questioning to enhance thinking aloud of strategies. Paired reading and peer tutoring where children take turns at taking the role of tutor, are found to be particularly helpful. Individualised learning programmes including computer-based programs are also available but they need to be selected in consultation with a professional in terms of suitability.

Instruction for children with LD can be either direct or a learning strategy instruction. Often teachers move from direct teacher mediated instruction with a lot of multimodal support and intensive practice to learning strategy and student mediated instruction. What is important is a focus on the individual, his strengths and needs and a programme that caters best to his profile, that is monitored frequently leading to upgradation of targets.

Teachers in countries like India where LD is not widely understood have the onus of explaining the nature of the problem to the parents and helping them to both understand and accept it. Regrettably given the 'straitjacket' nature of our school systems children with LD are likely to be total misfits. There is also not much scope for accessing alternate forms of education which will enable the child to circumvent his learning difficulty and yet achieve his innate potential. The only concession that has been provided for the LD child in India, as of date, is an exemption from having to learn two languages in addition to the medium of instruction. Legal provisions for some minimal facilities such as obtaining the aid of a writer are provided but are not easily accessed. Teachers have an important role in being proactive and ensuring that the child with LD is provided with alternates that will enable him to maximise his innate potential, despite the LD.

This brings us to some specific issues related to language and learning disability. The first major issue is the multilingual nature of our society and what it means for the child with LD. The second relates to the phenomenon of English being the most desired and widely used medium of instruction, at least in urban India. Finally we will end with a discussion of metalinguistics, which has shot into prominence in the area of reading acquisition and developmental reading disorders. These issues will be examined from the perspectives of our language and writing systems and their implications for the management of children with LD in this country.

India is a country of many languages and on an average most of us are exposed to at least three, a fact reflected in our official three-language policy as well as in our school curriculum. Often this means that the child speaks a particular language at home and much of his education takes place in a different language, often English. With the exception of a small percentage of the urban elite, most of our children struggle through the acquisition of this foreign language through their school years and at the same time cope with the content of what is taught, through this not too familiar medium. The additional burden that a situation like this poses on a typically developing child, let alone a child with LD, has become the focus of much recent research in Western countries, where a similar kind of bilingual situation is now emerging thanks to their large immigrant populations. The phenomenon now referred to as that of 'English as a second language' or ESL in countries like the USA; has led to special inputs being provided for children who learn English as a second language before mainstreaming them. Such provisions are regrettably not available in countries like ours. Further, unlike the bilingual child in the USA who gets substantial exposure to spoken English in his environment while learning to use it as a medium of instruction, this is not the case for our children. Despite being enrolled in schools with English as their medium of instruction, the exposure to good spoken English, which is absolutely essential to acquire the language, is seldom available to our children. Given the family backgrounds of many of these children, there is hardly any family input to language scaffolding and their acquisition and use of English is likely to be heavily influenced by their native language. This makes it doubly difficult for them when English is the medium of instruction. Students who come from a background with a familiarity with the language will clearly have an added advantage over those who do not. It is important to ensure that children have a language and communication proficiency that matches the learning-teaching style of the classroom. For those who do not, additional support in oral and written English should be provided before labelling them learning-disabled.

As children move to higher grades, the language of the classroom gradually becomes quite distinct from that used in everyday life. Students with communication disorders would require additional support to learn to use the language of the classroom with explicit language support and communication skill planning from a teacher who is understanding, enthusiastic and can effectively motivate and meet the needs of these children.

At times it could be difficult for the teacher to tell whether a given child has a learning disability or whether his difficulties are because of the bilingual background. A simple guideline is that the child with a disability or a communication disorder will exhibit the symptoms in both languages—the mother tongue and the medium of instruction.

During the last couple of decades there has been growing emphasis on the child's metalinguistic skills and his ability to master reading. Literacy acquisition it is said, is dependent on the child's metalinguistic ability, specifically phonological awareness.

The term metalinguistics has been variously defined as 'learning to treat language as a focus of cognitive reflection' or 'thinking about language to use language to think'. In the process of language acquisition, the child moves from the exclusive or greater use of non-linguistic skills in infancy to linguistic skills in the preschool years and then increasingly to the application of metalinguistic skills to become a proficient communicator. Metalinguistic skills therefore are seen as providing a link for moving children from social to increasingly instructional uses of language. It is also increasingly felt that though the overall aural-oral language skills of children with LD, specially the reading disabled, may fall in the normal range, they may have subtle or selective problems in some aspects of language acquisition that may affect their metalinguistic skills.

Among the metalinguistic skills, phonological awareness or the ability to consciously manipulate the phonemes or speech sounds of one's language is the first to emerge. In Western literature this skill has been linked to the ease with which a child masters reading and many of the recent assessment tools and intervention programs for reading disabled children in the west have focused on enhancing phonological awareness. A second area of metalinguistic skills that has drawn some attention is that of semantics. Children with LD are known to have marked word finding difficulties with limited vocabulary, fewer semantic associations and inefficient strategies for acquiring word meaning, which are bound to have an impact on their academics. Syntax or grammar has received comparatively lesser attention at the metalinguistic level. However it is acknowledged that since classroom discourses are typically informational and abstract, achieved through lexical density and complex syntactic constructions, any deficit in understanding and mastering this close relationship between form and function in language would impact academic learning.

As mentioned earlier, among the metalinguistic skills, phonological awareness and its relationship to literacy acquisition has received maximum attention in the West. At the same time some researchers also point out that this close relationship between phonological awareness and reading disability in the West may be at least in part due to the nature of the alphabetic writing systems, particularly opaque writing systems such as English in which the correspondence between the speech sounds and the small number of letters that represent them is not 'one to one'. Some studies in Eastern countries like India and Singapore suggest that the same does not apply to literacy acquisition in other types of writing systems as for instance those of India.

The writing systems of India whether of the Indo-Aryan North Indian languages like Hindi or the Dravidian South Indian languages like Kannada are much more explicit in terms of the letter to sound correspondence. This, however, has resulted in them being characterised by a large number of visually complex letters. Given the close correspondence between letter name and letter sound in the Indian languages, phonological awareness is not likely to be as crucial for literacy acquisition in these writing systems, an observation that has received empirical support. Hence while assessment of and intervention for phonological awareness may be important for Indian children learning to read and write in English, this may not be necessarily so for those who are learning to read and write in the vernacular. Instead they may require more acute visual processing skills in view of the larger set of visually complex letters. Paradoxically, under the influence of the Western literature we are teaching the Indian scripts through "phonics".

On the other hand, syntactic awareness may be more important for those of our children learning in the vernacular since unlike

Western languages like English our languages map on most of the grammatical markers like gender markers, tense markers, and prepositions, on to the root word itself, resulting in complex word formations within which the grammatical markers are embedded.

These differences in writing systems and languages bear important implications for the education and management of both the learning disabled child and the typically growing child in the regular classroom. Decisions on choice of medium of instruction, preschool literacy support and when and how the second and third languages are to be introduced to the child, have to be informed by knowledge of what is involved. It must be remembered that the mother tongue is learnt in natural situations where the child effortlessly masters the spoken form first and that the secondary written form is taught on the basis of the existing knowledge that the child possesses. The plasticity of the child's brain during the early years enhances the child's ability to learn more than one spoken language. Therefore the other tongue (English) should be introduced primarily as a spoken language in natural contexts recreated at school. The child can then gain equal or at least adequate competence in the spoken forms of both languages.

Ideally, reading of the Indian script should be introduced first, not only because the majority of children would have better competence in their mother tongue but also because despite their visual complexity, the Indian writing systems are transparent and once the child masters the script in a couple of years he can 'read' and 'write' pretty much anything. The teaching of writing should follow reading, not necessarily in parallel. There is a need to de-emphasise literacy skills in the early school years. Reading and writing of English can be introduced at a later stage, say the fourth grade (once the child has mastered spoken English and the script for the vernacular). Reading and writing of English can be focused on between the fourth to seventh grades and then depending on the subject taught, both languages can be used in parallel for both reading and writing—say literature and social sciences in the mother tongue, science and mathematics in English. It is time for us to develop innovative approaches that deal with the issues that confront us and maximise the benefits of our linguistic background in the interest of both the typically developing and the learning disabled child.

There is also a great need for assessment tools and intervention programmes to be made available in the vernacular. For the child with a learning disability it is crucial that decisions such as the choice of medium of instruction are made on the basis of a thorough evaluation of his strengths and weaknesses and an estimation of which language and script is likely to be the most facilitative.

Parental Support

Given the complexities of the situation, the only children with LD in India who have managed to circumvent their learning difficulties and achieve their potential, have been those with parents who have been sensitive to the needs of their child and managed to provide extensive and at times alternate supports during their school years. The few changes that have come about in terms of educational and legal provisions have also been the result of parental activism. Parental understanding and support will continue to be the most crucial factor in the successful education of children with LD. Nevertheless, with greater sensitivity on the part of the teacher and the society at large, the parental burdens can be ameliorated at least to some extent.

Section III

Other Communication Disorders

In this final section the reader will be introduced to the more grossly handicapping communication disorders such as those duc to hearing impairment and mental retardation, cerebral palsy and the autism spectrum disorders. In comparison with thc communication disorders described in the earlier sections, children with these disorders are likely to have more serious difficulties in communication. Many of them are likely to have such poor communication skills that they are generally out of the mainstream and are enrolled in special schools that specifically cater to their needs. However, mainstreaming and inclusive education for children with developmental disabilities, including those with severe communication disorders has been aggressively advocated in the West over the last three to four decades and has had some impact in India too.

In India the policy changes and provisions for inclusive education have been much more recent, with a trio of legislative initiatives made in the 1990s.Though the Persons with Disabilities Act passed in 1995 refers to equal opportunities, including access to mainstream schools for disabled children, very few children in reality, have had such access to mainstream education. Many schools do not even meet the quota of 3 per cent admissions for disabled children. When met, they are likely to be dominated by the orthopaedically handicapped. A new emphasis to integrating children with disabilities into regular school is now being made under the Sarva Shiksha Abhyan scheme. (See reading list in the appendix for more information on the various measures taken and provisions available, including educational provisions, for children with different types of handicaps). It is noteworthy that there is now a legislative and an administrative awareness of the educational needs and rights of children with developmental difficulties though the effects of these measures are taking time to trickle down and take root. Paradoxically, the debate has now come full circle in the West and teachers are now re-examining the feasibility of full integration, however well meaning it might be, in view of several issues that have cropped up ranging from the benefits and drawbacks to both the typically growing child in the classroom and to the child with the disability; to the pressures that the teachers are subjected to.

In a country like ours with its enormous population of young children, resulting in ever increasing pressures on the school system, the practicalities of integration have to be even more carefully considered. It is undeniable that the child with a disability has as great a right to education as his non-disabled peer. Yet in providing for this right it is also important to ensure that the child is indeed exercising his right for the best possible education given his circumstances. There can therefore not be a blanket rule for all children with disabilities. The decision for integration or not, has to be taken jointly by the parents and the school authorities, considering all relevant factors in each individual instance with the goal in each case being, maximising the potential of each individual child.

Children with developmental language disorders such as those caused by hearing impairment, cerebral palsy and mental retardation learn language in the same sequence as their normally developing peers, but the pace is delayed. The child will not 'outgrow' these language delays and needs special early intervention and long-term support to achieve his fullest potential. The communication disorder not only affects them in understanding others and making themselves understood, but also often interferes with their abilities to learn and compose their thoughts and ideas. However, when given good support many of them can lead full, normal lives.

With the recent increase in the incidence of pervasive developmental disorders there is a need to be aware of and understand this complex group of disorders. An entire chapter will therefore be devoted to introducing this group of developmental disorders. The variety of Autistic Spectrum Disorders (ASD) ranging from those which are mild in nature and yet interfere in the overall development of the child, to those which are of late onset such as Asperger's syndrome and will progressively interfere with the child's social development will be dealt with in Chapter 11. The final chapter will deal with a variety of syndromic disorders in which speech-language and communication skills can be affected.

8
Hearing Impairment

Hearing impairment occurs frequently in children, both independently and as a component in children with multiple developmental disabilities. It may be present at birth or acquired later. While mild or transient hearing impairments during the developmental years do not as a rule affect language development, when the hearing impairment is present at birth or is acquired in infancy and is severe in degree it often results in developmental language disorders. Hearing loss can be suspected when a child does not consistently respond to being called by his name, frequently misunderstands speech or asks the speaker to repeat, or responds better when the speaker is facing him. Hearing impairment may affect one or both ears. A child, whose hearing is affected only in one ear, will have a tendency to turn his better ear towards the source of sound or will respond better when spoken to from that direction.

Definition

The human ear can respond to sounds across a specific frequency range and degrees of loudness. A sound is measured for its loudness in units called decibels (dBs) and for its frequency or pitch in units called hertz (Hz). Hearing loss is described as mild, moderate, severe or profound depending on the loudness level at which the person responds to sounds in the 'speech frequency range' or the frequencies which are associated with human speech. Normal hearing is characterised by the ability to respond to sounds in the speech range, that is 500 to 4000Hz, at a loudness level of 0-15 dB in both ears. When a child requires the loudness level to be higher than this for the perception of sound, he can be suspected of having a hearing loss. Those with hearing thresholds of upto 90 dB, in one or both ears are generally referred to as being hearing impaired. Those with hearing thresholds of 90 dB or above, in both the ears are categorised as having severe or profound hearing loss and are often referred to as being deaf. Deafness is viewed as a condition in which the child can barely perceive sound whereas a child with a hearing impairment or loss can perceive some auditory stimuli including speech. Deafness interferes in the child's ability to acquire spoken language with or without amplification. At times the terms 'hearing impaired' and 'deaf' are used synonymously. When a child is deaf, auditory-verbal communication is difficult or impossible without amplification.

Incidence and Prevalence

Precise estimates of the incidence and prevalence of hearing impairment are hard to come by since hearing loss may be congenital or acquired, it can be mild to severe, in one or both ears and can be seen in individuals of all ages. The universal figures for the incidence of congenital hearing loss are 1-6 per 1000 live births. Western surveys suggest that about 5 per cent of the school going population has some kind of hearing impairment. This includes those in special schools and those who are mainstreamed into regular school. In India it is estimated that of every 1, 00,000 children below the age of 5 years, there are 55 children who have severe to profound hearing loss.

Characteristics

Hearing impairments are often described as a 'hidden deficit' as they are not obvious to the eye. However there are several characteristics that are exhibited by children with hearing impairments. Delayed onset of speech and language is one of the most common consequences of a hearing loss. Persisting difficulties such as inconsistent responses to sounds and speech, including responses to being called, or to verbal instructions; watching the speaker's face closely or asking for repetitions of questions and instructions are often characteristic of children with hearing impairment. They may also speak too softly or too loudly (depending on the type of hearing loss) or appear inattentive, dull and uninterested in group interactions. They often have poor language and perform particularly poorly in subjects that are dependent on verbal learning and literacy skills such as the languages and social science classes. Their speech may be unclear with parts of words (beginning and endings) dropped. Children with a hearing loss affecting only one ear may have particular difficulty in localising sound or locating where the sound is coming from. They are particularly likely to show inconsistency and difficulty in listening in noisy environments. They may seem inattentive in specific communication situations. The communication difficulties of children with hearing impairment often affect their social development and they may seem emotionally immature and naïve. As a result their interpersonal and family relationships may also be affected.

Disorders

Hearing loss is classified in different ways. One commonly accepted classification is based on when the hearing loss was present, i.e., whether it was present at birth (congenital) or later (acquired). It may also be classified as unilateral or bilateral depending on whether only one ear is affected or both.

Hearing impairment may also be classified on the basis of the type of hearing loss, that is on the basis of which part of the auditory system is affected. According to this classification, there are four types of hearing loss – conductive, sensorineural, mixed hearing loss and central hearing loss. Briefly, conductive hearing losses are those in which the sound is not conducted efficiently through the outer and middle ear, resulting in it being muffled.

Conductive hearing losses are frequently a consequence of middle ear infections, are less severe in nature and can be treated medically or surgically. Sensorineural hearing losses are consequent to damage to the inner ear. They are more severe in nature and cannot be treated medically or surgically. Children with sensorineural hearing loss invariably have their speech-language development affected and have to use amplification devices such as hearing aids. When an individual has defects in the outer and middle ear, as well in the inner ear, the combination of a conductive and sensorineural hearing loss, it is termed a mixed hearing loss. A central hearing loss on the other hand refers to hearing impairment that is caused by damage to the nerve pathways to the brain or the brain itself.

Causes

Hearing loss may be caused by a wide range of factors. While severe congenital hearing loss seen at birth is often due to genetic factors, other factors such as maternal infection during pregnancy, chronic ear infections or viral and bacterial infections such as meningitis may also lead to hearing loss. Hearing impairment may also result as a consequence of prolonged exposure to high doses of medication or injuries such as head injuries. At times hearing loss may be caused by exposure to loud noise. In the recent past an increasing number of children are seen to have difficulties in the processing of speech due to subtle disorders in auditory processing. Finally in a small number of children, hearing loss or impairment may be functional in nature, that is, they are caused by psychological rather than biological factors. In an even smaller number, the hearing loss may be due to malingering or conscious pretension for some perceived advantage.

Referral and Assessments

While some hearing impairments, particularly the conductive and mixed hearing losses can be treated medically or surgically, most other hearing impairments cannot be treated or cured, resulting in a permanent deficit. In these instances treatment takes the form of alternate measures such as the provision of suitable amplificatory devices based on a thorough assessment of the type and degree of hearing loss.

The degree and type of hearing impairment is arrived at on the basis of extensive audiological assessments which range from behavioural assessment of hearing in the young infant by observing infant response to calibrated signals, to automated electro-physiological procedures to test adequacy of inner ear and auditory nerve function called tests of auditory brain stem response (ABR). The diagnosis of the type of hearing impairment is based on matching the personal medical history to the configuration of the audiogram and the results of the various special tests. Large scale screening tests are popular for the identification of hearing impairment in school going children. A child who fails the screening test is then followed up in the audiological clinic with more extensive testing under conditions that are controlled for environmental noise.

Subsequent to the identification and assessment of a hearing loss, wherever feasible, medical and surgical procedures are considered. When such an option is not available, the child is assessed for and fitted with a suitable amplification device, to help him cope with the hearing loss and its consequences.

Intervention

There has long been a bitter divide over the issue of what is the best line of action in the rehabilitation of severely hearing impaired or deaf children. Some have argued that the deaf child should be trained in an easier mode of communication such as sign language. Others are of the opinion that this would socially isolate the deaf child and result in a separate 'deaf culture'. The latter have therefore argued that the best mode of intervention is to provide the deaf child with an amplification device and train him in the language of his community, however difficult this may seem. It is now conceded that no one system of communication is right for all deaf children. Increasingly the choice of communication mode is made on an individual basis, considering the degree and type of hearing loss, the resources that are available for training in both modes, and the informed choice of the family.

Auditory amplification through devices such as hearing aids can be extremely valuable for a sizable proportion of the hearing impaired and can aid substantially in the acquisition of language through the aural-oral mode. However, there are those in whom even with amplification there is not enough hearing for the acquisition of speech or verbal language. In such instances, visual communication modes such as sign language, finger spelling and cued speech are employed to enable the child to communicate in an alternate mode. Combinations of methods are also advocated in an approach known as 'total communication'. In this chapter we will focus on hearing impaired children who are fitted with hearing aids and trained in the aural-oral approach.

Hearing aids can be of different types. They can be worn on the body, behind the ear or in the ear. It is important to understand that unlike spectacles, which enable the user to see effectively when worn and on the whole do not need a period of getting used to, hearing aids do not immediately serve the user in the same manner. The amplification of sound through a hearing aid is not selective, as they amplify all the sounds in the environment resulting in a feeling akin to having a loudspeaker in the ear. However, with technological improvements, newer hearing aids are now able to selectively amplify the sounds in the frequency range that the particular user is facing difficulty in. Still it needs getting used to and the hearing aid user will require some time to acclimatise to the aid.

During the last couple of decades, efforts have also been made to develop alternate types of aids such as tactile aids and vibrators to enable the hearing impaired to communicate better. Of these, the cochlear implants have been the most successful and are increasingly popular. Cochlear implants are electrical devices that provide electrical stimulation directly to the cochlea or the inner ear through electrodes that are embedded surgically. An external microphone picks up the sound and passes it on to an external speech processor (which is like a miniaturized computer). The speech processor analyses and digitises the sounds into coded signals, which are then passed on to the cochlear implant. The activations of the internal electrodes provide electrical stimulation to the undamaged remaining nerve fibres and are sent on to the brain along the auditory pathway.

When cochlear implants were first tried out in the last decade of the twentieth century they were primarily tried on adults with acquired hearing impairment. Since then they have been increasingly used with young children with congenital hearing loss (even as young as two years of age) and provide useful hearing and improved communication abilities. While cochlear implants facilitate the perception of sound it must be remembered that the child has to learn to interpret these sound patterns and identify speech. It does not making hearing normal. It provides a different kind of sound perception and the user has to get used to it and will need some training and support in learning to do so, as well as long term monitoring. Further they are expensive and are not always successful. Factors such as the efficacy of the implanted electrodes in stimulating the surviving elements of an individual's damaged auditory nerve, status of the cochlea, age of onset of deafness, age at implantation, duration of deafness and the effectiveness of education and /or rehabilitation can influence the success of the cochlear implant.

Other than the cochlear implant, a variety of other devices such as text telephones are now being developed to assist the hearing impaired individual.

Rehabilitation for the child with severe hearing impairment or deafness begins with auditory skill training, after the fitting of an appropriate amplificatory device. This includes training the child to detect sounds, discriminate, imitate, integrate and comprehend them. There is also an enormous amount of incidental learning that takes place through audition. The hearing impaired child has to be provided training in auditory skills through familiarisation, contrast, highlighting and repetition, across distances and environments that vary in background noise.

Speech reading (lip reading) is used as an adjunct to auditory training in the rehabilitation of a child with hearing impairment.

It enhances the child's ability to perceive the facial and articulatory movements during speech production and uses these as compensatory cues to comprehend speech in the absence of adequate auditory perception of the speech stream. Both these methods, that is, auditory training and speech reading are used to complement each other to enhance the child's communication skills.

In the auditory verbal approach to rehabilitation, for children who have some hearing, the emphasis is on training the child to learn to listen and providing the child with the opportunity of being educated in a regular classroom alongside with his peers; eventually leading to full integration into the hearing world. Ideal as this may be, there are several factors such as the type and severity of hearing loss, age of onset, age at identification, type of hearing aid used, frequency and duration of hearing aid usage, quality of subsequent management including family support and availability of professional services; which will influence the outcome in this approach to rehabilitation of the hearing impaired.

School Support

Since the latter half of the twentieth century many children with hearing impairments in Western countries have been integrated into regular classrooms along with support services. As a rule these children are in regular school for the whole day from the age of 4-5 years and receive additional support for language development and communication skills. The decision to mainstream or not, is dependent on the combined effect of several factors such as degree and type of hearing loss, age of onset, age of identification, age at which intervention was received, extent of benefit from hearing aid, cognitive abilities, additional impairments, parental and family support, and the availability or access to different services.

A major concern in integrating deaf children into regular classrooms is their communication skill. Invariably children with hearing impairment are slow to acquire speech and language and need special support to do so. When conditions for early identification and intervention are met they can follow a normal course of language acquisition like their hearing peers, but at a slower rate. However, even those with good language skills tend to have deficits in higher language acquisition and show subtle deficits in the more complex grammatical constructions and in pragmatic skills. They tend to depend on the context for cohesion in communication. Increasingly access to literacy skills is being provided early and has been found to have a beneficial effect on communication skills.

Language acquisition and development are significantly affected in most children with moderate to profound hearing loss. Though the hearing impairment itself does not affect the intelligence of the child, lack of or delay in the development of an adequate communication system may lead to an implication of a low estimate of intelligence. In order to help the child achieve his basic intellectual potential, in addition to early and regular auditory training and speech-language therapy from a specialist, the hearing impaired child often requires the assistance of a special educator to attain adequate education.

The classroom teacher also plays a vital role in the integration of the hearing impaired child in a regular classroom. It is important for teachers to work together with the child's audiologist and SLP to teach the child to use his or her residual hearing to the maximum extent possible. Familiarity of the teacher with basic care and trouble shooting of the hearing aid is necessary. While placing the child in the classroom, the teacher also needs to take into consideration factors such as how best to optimise the distance between speaker and listener, facilitate visual communication, provide clear speech and generally enhance strategies for improving listening skills. Maximal facilitation for integration of a hearing impaired child in a regular classroom also necessitates taking into consideration class room changes to enhance classroom acoustics and the use of amplification devices such as FM systems but may not generally be feasible in Indian conditions.

Taking care of simple factors such as providing favourable seating where the hearing impaired child can better lip read his teacher or seating him in such a way that his better ear is turned towards the teacher and his classmates, can go a long way in facilitating the child's classroom participation. The teacher should take care to face the hearing impaired child while speaking and have his/her face (teacher's face) well lit with the mouth clearly visible. The teacher should also speak clearly at a normal rate of speech. Writing new words on boards, providing notes prior to the class and subtitles for visuals will help. The child may also have particular difficulty in sourcing the sound, when audiovisuals such as tapes and videos are used in teaching, and extra care should be taken during these presentations. In classroom discussions pointing to the speaker, repeating questions and comments and controlling the pace of discussion will ensure that the hearing impaired child will also fully participate in such discussions. Further the hearing impaired child may need additional cues to topics and topic changes, in order to ensure that he is not left out of discussions. The knowledge of the topic is essential for the child's greater participation. Large classroom discussions where the topic can change swiftly can be particularly difficult for the hearing impaired child. It demands greater concentration as the many words look alike and the child has both to listen to the speaker and watch his lip movements, making it a tiring process. Dictation can also be difficult for the same reason.

The teacher should also remember that unlike the typical child in the classroom, the deaf child has to both learn language and learn through language. They gather less information about the environment than their normal hearing peers and have greater difficulty in interactive communication. Talking to the child about what interests him, encouraging questions and initiation of dialogues help. So does providing expansions and clarifications of a child's intended meaning and providing more time for him to reply. The teacher should avoid the overuse of questions that can be answered with a simple yes or no.

A common failure on the part of adults who deal with children with hearing impairment, including therapists and teachers, is the excessive use of adult directed speech. It is important to be aware of and sensitive to the need for enhancing communication that is both personal and instructional. These must include discussing experiences that are personal to the child, and communication on topics that are chosen by the child and not adult directed. The hearing impaired child should be consistently and conscientiously provided with abundant speaking and listening opportunities. Given the difficulties in their listening skills, they need to be taught to request for clarifications and repetitions when there is a communication breakdown. With intensive, interactive, meaningful listening and speaking practice throughout his school years the hearing impaired child can take his rightful place in society.

Reading and writing can enhance the language and communication skills of hearing impaired children and literacy acquisition should be encouraged at an early stage. Apart from aiding the child in communication skills and classroom curricular content, the classroom teacher can also play an important role in the child's personal and social development. Children with hearing impairment are often naïve, have poor self esteem and find social interactions difficult. The teacher needs to actively seek and support their social and group participation. The average child learns to organise his thinking and regulate his social contact as he acquires the complexities and subtleties of the use of language. The hearing impaired child needs specific assistance and direction for the same. The teacher can integrate these social skill lessons into classroom activities and lessons and model the same. Along with instilling in him a sense of responsibility for himself and his studies he might also need additional support in dealing with classroom bullies. This does not however mean that he should be overprotected. Despite the many odds that the child with a hearing impairment faces, an understanding and positive teacher can be the most crucial factor in determining whether a child with hearing impairment integrates successfully or not.

Curricular modifications may also be required to adapt to the specific needs of the deaf child. Children with normal hearing have considerable mastery over their language, by the time they enrol in school. Their communication skills by this time are adequate to meet their basic needs and to exchange social pleasantries, appropriate for their age. At school they are introduced to literacy skills and to increasingly use language and communication for knowledge building. The hearing impaired child, on the other hand, generally has inadequate language and communication skills in comparison with his peers at school entry age and has to continue to make special efforts in order to cope with the acquisition and use of language. Simultaneously he has to cope with the literacy and knowledge based skills that he is introduced to at school. As he goes to higher grades, teaching and learning become more and more language based and even the smallest lag in linguistic development can seriously jeopardise his academic achievements. This is even more so in current day Indian schools where a large number of children are taught by a single teacher, more or less exclusively, through the verbal mode and very little participatory or interactive learning. Consequently, curricular modifications may be required to adapt to the special needs of the hearing impaired child in the regular classroom. These curricular modifications may include language exemptions, restructuring of the curriculum and adaptation of teaching and evaluation strategies.

In view of their specific difficulties in language acquisition, exemption from the three language formula recommended for all children in regular schools has now been made available to hearing impaired children in several states. This does not mean that a hearing impaired child cannot learn more than one language if he so desires, as some do. However, if the child with a hearing impairment continues to struggle with language acquisition s/he has the choice of dropping the second or third language without affecting his academic career.

Adaptations may also need to be made in syllabus, teaching and evaluation strategies for the hearing impaired at various levels of schooling. At the preschool level, the emphasis is generally on acquisition of communication skills including listening skills, speech reading and accurate speech production, language learning emphasising specific linguistic aspects such as the appropriate use of grammatical markers and adequate language use, employing special techniques that are particularly suitable to the hearing impaired. At the primary and high school level the emphasis is on classroom requirements, syllabus modifications and adaptation of teaching and evaluation strategies, with continued monitoring of adequacy of language skills. Hearing impaired children perform better with participatory learning that involve a lot of visuals rather than with language based learning. It is important to use simple straight forward language in instructing them and ensuring that the instructions have indeed been understood. At the same time, increasingly importance is given to early literacy acquisition for the hearing impaired, as early and adequate literacy exposure can often help them to alleviate some of the difficulties faced in verbal language learning. Mathematics and problem solving need to be taught with visual and kinaesthetic cues rather than verbal cues. Computer assisted language learning and academic learning are increasingly being employed to enable the hearing impaired child to circumlocute the verbal and academic difficulties caused by the hearing loss. Academic evaluation for the hearing impaired child also has to be more frequent and individualistic with flexibility in time and mode of testing.

In the West, alternate modes of communication such as sign language and total communication are often used in regular classrooms in which hearing impaired children are integrated. In fact in a major attitudinal change, normally hearing children are given credits for learning sign language as an additional language. The services of an interpreter for those students who use sign language are often made available in regular schools and at public forums. For those who are trained in both aural-oral methods and a visual mode such as sign language, finger spelling and cued speech, a choice of method is made available.

The general constraints of a large population and the large number of children in classrooms with inadequate teachers, a poor teacher- child ratio, lack of adequate space and infrastructure are indeed major hurdles to successful integration of hearing impaired children in the regular classroom in India today. At the same time a well informed and empathic teacher can go a long way in empowering the parents of the hearing impaired child and with their help enable the child to maximise his/her potential

Parental Support

For the parents of a child with a hearing impairment, the support that tney are required to provide their child, from infancy to adulthood, is a long and arduous journey. Ultimately the confidence with which their child becomes a part of his larger society depends on the early, intensive and sustained support they provide. Professionals and teachers become a part of this parental endeavour by contributing to it in a suitable manner and at appropriate times. An understanding of these issues, followed by close cooperation and continuous monitoring by all concerned are the most essential elements for a successful outcome.

9
Mental Retardation

Mental retardation refers to conditions in which children are slow in acquiring developmental skills across the board, that is, in most physical and mental functions, as compared to their peers. It can be caused by a variety of factors and ranges from mild to severe in degree. While those with severe retardation are more in need of rehabilitatory services, a large number of children with mild to moderate mental retardation can be enrolled in regular schools and can optimise their functional skills.

Definition

Definitions of mental retardation emphasise that it is not a disease but a condition which is characterised by 'significant limitations both in intellectual functioning and in adaptive behaviour as expressed in conceptual, social, and practical adaptive skills' and that it begins in childhood. It is a developmental disability that is defined by intellectual functioning, generally as measured by standard tests of intelligence. Children with mental retardation function well below average intellectually, in comparison with their peers, and have significant limitations in daily living skills.

However, it is important to understand that mental retardation has many dimensions and that it can be affected positively by good and prolonged support. The intellectual limitations must be considered within the context of the individual's environment—personal, social and cultural, and not on the basis of standard measures alone. Assessments of intellectual performance on intelligence tests can be influenced by cultural and linguistic diversity, as well as other factors such as sensory and motor issues. Some children with mental retardation may have certain strengths too. When these are taken into consideration and personalised support provided over a prolonged period of time, beginning in early childhood, the functioning of the child with mental retardation will improve in aspects such as self help, independence, social relationships and participation in school and community, including holding a job and living independently.

Incidence and Prevalence

Reports on prevalence rates of mental retardation vary in their estimates, ranging from 1 per cent to 2.5-3 per cent of the general population. In India the prevalence rate is said to be about 3 per cent with a higher prevalence in rural areas than urban. Reported rates are higher among children than adults and this could be due to the gains made in saving children with high risk or due to higher mortality rates among mentally retarded children. It is more common in males than females with a ratio of 1.5:1. It is to be found in all cultures, socioeconomic, educational, racial and ethnic groups.

Characteristics

In understanding mental retardation it is important to know that mental retardation is different from mental illness. The term retardation refers to slowness and mental retardation is therefore mental slowness and not mental illness. The characteristics of mental retardation listed below will make this clear.

Children with congenital (at birth) mental retardation are slower in attaining their developmental milestones as compared with their peers. This delay is seen both in motor development such as sitting, standing and walking and in mental functions such as language. If on the other hand, mental retardation is a consequence of illnesses such as encephalitis or meningitis or injuries, the developmental milestones would be normal up to the time of the injury or illness and subsequently may slow down or even regress. The lag in development should be present before the age of 18 years for the term mental retardation (MR) to be applied.

The most characteristic sign of MR is that the functioning of the child in several developmental areas is not on par with others of his age, from the same sociocultural background and community. Unlike children with communication and learning disorders where the deficit is specific to communication and learning, in the case of children with MR, there is a generalised impairment in intellectual development and adaptive functioning. However, children with MR may have communication and learning delays and disorders over and above those warranted by the mental retardation. That is, some children with MR may not communicate even at the level expected of children of their mental age. They may also have other speech disorders such as poor articulation coexisting with delay in language acquisition.

Children with mild mental retardation may not be identified in the preschool years as the delays in their milestones may not be gross enough to attract attention. However, in the formal environment of the school they may be seen to have difficulties with social, communication and functional academic skills. Their overall language development is similar to their typically developing peers, but at a slower rate and this applies to both receptive and expressive language skills. Their comprehension and expressive lexical development lags behind their peers. Their speech is often characterised by poor articulation and poor expressive syntax, resulting in poor speech intelligibility. In some specific subtypes such as Down syndrome, the voice is distinctively different—often rough, breathy and low-pitched. Syntax or acquisition of grammar appears to be particularly difficult for children with MR. Some children with MR appear relatively proficient in word recognition skills, but by and large have poor decoding skills that affect their reading and literacy acquisition. Children with MR also use less sophisticated play than their peers in everyday life.

The condition of mental retardation is often associated with other disabilities including visual and hearing deficits. Frequently hearing loss is found in some children with MR, particularly in subtypes such as those with Down syndrome. A substantial proportion of children with mental retardation suffer from epilepsy. They may also have accompanying motor or speech deficits. Children with mental retardation are generally gregarious and friendly without too many behavioural issues. However, at times, aggression, self-injurious behaviour and mood swings may also be present. These may be related to causative factors, for instance if the mental retardation is caused by a head injury, it may also cause a personality change. Disorders such as attention deficits, hyperactivity and stereotypic movements may also be seen in some children with MR.

Disorders

Formal diagnoses of mental retardation are made on the basis of a given child's performance on a standardised test of intellectual functioning and are expressed either as an intelligence quotient (IQ) or as a mental age (MA). For a diagnosis of MR it is important that onset is before 18 years of age. Mental retardation is defined as an IQ score below 70–75 with IQ scores of around 100 being considered normal. A variety of Western tests for assessment of IQ are available (e.g., Wechsler Intelligence Scales for Children, Stanford-Binet Intelligence Scale, Kaufman Assessment Battery for Children).Some of them have been adapted for use in the Indian context (Binet-Kamath Test of Intelligence). It is important that the test administered is suited to the individuals' sociocultural background, native language and associated handicaps including communication difficulties, as well as motor and sensory handicaps. In addition, the motivation and cooperation of the subject can affect test results. Specialised tests may also be used to measure other specific aspects of development

Children with mental retardation are often classified into sub groups based on the severity of the MR. One of the most widely used systems the Diagnostic and Statistical Manual of Mental Disorders, Fourth Edition (DSM-IV) classifies MR into four different degrees of mild, moderate, severe, and profound, based on the functioning level of the individual. Children with IQ scores in the ranges from 50–75 are classified as mildly mentally retarded. They constitute nearly 85 per cent of the mentally retarded population and these are children who are likely to be enrolled in regular schools. They can often acquire some basic academic skills and become fairly self sufficient in independent living with family and social support. About 10 per cent of the mentally retarded population have IQ scores between 35 and 55 and are classified as having moderate MR. They can be trained to carry out basic self care and some simple work that they can do under supervision. They generally acquire some communication skills but are unable to achieve independent living and have to be supported in extended family or community set ups. About 1–5 per cent of those with MR have IQ scores less than 30–40 and are classified as having severe to profound degrees of retardation. These children often have other complicating factors and are unlikely to be brought to a regular educational set up. They can be trained in some basic self care skills in an environment that provides high levels of structure and supervision.

It is the child with mild, and perhaps in some instances one with moderate MR that the teacher in the regular classroom is likely to be faced with. As a rule, these children develop social and communication skills in their preschool years and do not show marked impairment in sensorimotor areas. As a result they are not distinguishable from their peers until a later age when their difficulties in academic skills become more pronounced.

Since they are capable of achieving social and vocational skills adequate for self support, it is important that they are provided with the opportunity to achieve this potential with appropriate support.

Adaptive functioning is of key importance in the long-term management of those with MR. Adaptive functioning refers to an individual's capacity to deal with the everyday environment in a manner that is expected of someone of their age in their particular sociocultural background and community setting. It comprises the social, conceptual and practical skills that are required from individuals on a day to day basis. Children with MR who do not receive adequate stimulation, exposure and training in their home and school environments are impacted negatively in terms of their adaptive functioning across several skill areas such as communication, self care, social and interpersonal skills. Educational, social and vocational opportunities have a definite effect on maximising the adaptive functioning of children with mental retardation enabling them to respond at their best in day to day situations in their environment.

Causes

Mental retardation can be caused by a variety of factors, largely biological. Among the biological factors are the genetic factors, which include inherited abnormalities such as the fragile X syndrome, inborn errors of metabolism such as phenylketonuria, genetic mutations such as trisomy 18 and 21 or Down syndrome. Other biological factors that can result in MR are prenatal illnesses and complications, which include maternal illnesses and infections during pregnancy as well as maternal drug and alcohol intake, or smoking. Childhood illnesses such as meningitis and encephalitis or any other major infection that is not treated immediately and adequately, or injuries such as head trauma may also cause mental retardation.

In addition to these biological factors, MR can also be caused by environmental and psychosocial factors such as lack of stimulation, inadequate nutrition, and exposure to toxins such as lead. Children who are neglected and not provided with mental and physical stimulation may suffer long-term learning difficulties despite being born healthy and normal. Children who live in poverty and suffer from malnutrition, unhealthy living conditions, and improper or inadequate medical care are also at a higher risk. Basic nutrition and living conditions with mental and physical stimulation are as important for normal development as being born healthy and normal. While these biological and social-environmental factors have been identified as potential causes of MR, the precise cause of MR in each and every child is not always identifiable.

Referral and Assessment

Prior to intervention for children with mental retardation, a complete medical examination and provision of medical intervention when warranted, is essential. This applies to the assessment and management of associated problems that are often seen in conjunction with MR. In the majority of cases with mental retardation, however, medical intervention is not possible. When this is so, a thorough assessment by a multidisciplinary team of specialists such as psychologists, speech-language pathologists and occupational therapists should be carried out to determine the potential of the child along with current functional levels. A comprehensive intervention programme can then be planned addressing the varied needs of the individual child. This may include speech-language therapy, occupational therapy and daily living skills development as well as behavioural and social skills training.

Intervention

Subsequent to the evaluation, intervention should be provided as early as possible. It is now clear that early intervention including full inclusion in preschool and elementary school has beneficial effects on the long-term outcome. Individuals with mild to moderate retardation can acquire adequate skills for independent living and this can be achieved only by providing timely and consistent family, educational, community, social and vocational support.

In the West where services for individuals with mental retardation were initiated in a systematic manner much earlier than in India, all children with mental retardation are entitled to free and appropriate education. Children with MR are provided with many facilities such as a choice of educational placements ranging from special schools to general education and a host of options where they can combine these in different proportions such as provision of special services in an inclusive classroom. The emphasis is on integration to the extent possible, along with assistance in transition from school to higher education or vocational training in the later years. Depending on the degree of retardation the child may be placed in a regular school alone or in a regular school with a resource room. Alternately, they may be enrolled in schools with special classes or special schools, particularly if the degree of mental retardation is moderate or severe.

Such a change in approach to the education of the disabled has only recently been witnessed in India. Since the latter half of the twentieth century, the government of India through its different departments is increasingly providing incentives for inclusive education of the disabled, including the mentally retarded. So for instance, while the department of Education provides institutional aid for schools that integrate disabled children by way of allowances for books and stationery, transport and escort allowance as well as for aids and equipment, the department of Personnel and Training provides for an educational allowance to disabled children and reimbursement of the tuition fee. Scholarships for disabled children integrated in regular schools, are also made available. Further the government of India has set up the National Institute of Mental Health in Secunderabad which functions as a nodal agency for all round benefit of individuals with MR, including teacher training.

The approach to therapeutic management of children with mental retardation has over the years changed from a strictly behaviouristic approach to more natural approaches such as milieu teaching, in keeping with the goals of integration, independent living and enhancement of adaptive functioning. Communication deficits, in particular developmental language deficits which are over and above those that can be accounted for by the cognitive, motor and /or sensory deficits of the children, are often seen in children with MR and have to be specifically targeted if the goals of integration and independent living are to be achieved. A communication deficit will affect all aspects of the child's life including social and educational opportunities and the eventual outcome in terms of independent living. Intervention for the same will depend on the nature of the deficit (articulatory versus syntax) as well as the mismatch between the expectation based on cognitive capabilities and actual performance. It will also include selective strategies for teaching reading and contextual rehearsals and is best done under the guidance of a trained SLP. Alternate modes of communication such as manual communication and or signing may also be recommended in the case of individuals with specific oromotor deficits

In addition to the supportive services provided by therapists and the classroom teacher, children with MR often need support from a special educator. Here too, the focus has shifted from providing general support in achieving academic goals per se, to enhancing adaptive skills that will come handy in achieving independent living. They include conceptual skills such as handling money and self management; social skills such as building self esteem and handling interpersonal relations, taking responsibility for oneself and one's actions and following social rules; and practical skills such as self-help skills of daily living, basic house keeping and self care. These are generally achieved through individualised support plans, which take into account the individual's capacities and limitations, as well as his age and sociocultural milieu.

School Support

It is quite common that slow learners and teachable mentally retarded children remain undetected in the regular school particularly in the early school years. The classroom teacher has an important role in identifying children whose condition may have been undetected and in making the appropriate referrals. The teacher needs to be able to suggest additional assessments to clarify the issue and discuss the matter with the parents without employing any derogatory labels and within a positive and optimistic outlook.

Apart from playing a role in identification and referral, where necessary, there are strategies that can be used by the classroom teacher to enhance the development of the child with mental retardation in the regular classroom. It begins by acknowledging the fact that a disability exists, thereby paving the way for the acceptance of the child by his peers. A second important factor is not to shy away from discussing the functional difficulties and needs of the child directly, but in privacy. The teacher sets the model for good communication with the disabled child by making the atmosphere conducive to easy and good interactive communication. The child with MR will need encouragement and assistance in participating in all classroom activities and discussions. Patience, acceptance and understanding on the part of the teacher will set the tone for the classroom atmosphere. It is important to give a patient listening to children with MR and allow them more time to complete their activities. The student with MR should be placed in relative proximity to the teacher. It is also the teacher's responsibility to keep up the motivation of the child with MR, through positive reinforcement whenever appropriate, providing opportunities to participate and ensuring a measure of success.

Academic areas that may be difficult for the child with MR should be anticipated and additional support provided. The learning readiness of the child needs to be ascertained. Complex tasks need to be broken into simple steps. Concrete explanations and learning by doing are more valuable for the child with MR. While verbal rehearsals, drill and repetition further support learning in the MR child, it is also true that they benefit from the play way and the multisensorial approach. Alternate methods of attaining the same objective should be explored and all success reinforced positively. A judicious and complementary use of these diverse methods will bring the best results.

Special consideration should also be paid to classroom organisation and scheduling time for children with MR in the regular classroom, as they are likely to require more time than their peers to catch up with them and master learning. Small group instructions, peer tutoring and programmed instructions have also been found to be helpful. The curriculum should be graded and adapted to the needs of the child with MR and introduced in a systematic and sequential manner. Frequent repetitions with periods of short duration are also more suited to the child with MR. In addition the child with MR, unlike his typically growing peer, has to be taught specifically how to process information. For the mentally retarded child with physical limitations the use of appropriate aids and appliances should also be explored, with the involvement of the family.

Academic evaluations and assessments are also difficult for the child with MR. Continuous assessment during the school year is preferable to scheduled examinations. Testing through the optimal mode, with provision of extra time to complete the test should be considered. Legal provision for writers is now allowed in some states. Attempts should be made to provide any additional assistance that the child may need. With individualised support in key areas, children with mental retardation can grow to live an independent and fruitful life. The school environment and support from the regular classroom teacher will go a long way in making this possible.

As a society, it is our responsibility to ensure that the teachable mentally retarded child should be identified early and included in the universalisation of primary education. This is important not only from the humanitarian point of view, but also in terms of practicality in the long run, to reduce the economic burden on society of supporting unproductive individuals. The community therefore has a responsibility in mainstreaming children with mental retardation to thc extent possible in order to provide them with a reality orientation. The overall aim of education for the child with MR should target not only academic skills but also social competence, personal adjustment and occupational adequacy.

Parental Support

The eventual status of a child with mental retardation is largely dependent upon the quality and duration of the support that he or she receives from the family, particularly in view of the meagre support and alternates provided by the government agencies. Many non-governmental agencies and parental associations have made remarkable contributions in this area. The setting up of the National Trust for Welfare of Persons with Autism, Cerebral Palsy, Mental Retardation and Multiple Disabilities, by the Government of India, has finally provided them with a forum that can provide a platform for their grievances, address their concerns and coordinate their activities at a national level.

10

Cerebral Palsy

Most of us have seen children who have extreme difficulty in controlling the movements of their body and consequently seem contorted, with poor posture; the lack of motor control affecting most of their skills in day to day life. This condition known as cerebral palsy is a movement disorder caused by damage to the brain, before, during or soon after birth and can range from mild to severe. It is a lifelong condition in that it cannot be medically cured, but at the same time it is not a disease nor does it increase progressively. With therapy, education, and the use of assistive technological aids, the child with cerebral palsy or CP can go on to lead a productive life.

Definition

The term cerebral palsy (CP) is an umbrella term that refers to a subgroup of children with developmental disabilities that are characterised by disorders of movement and posture, which often persist across the lifespan of the individual. Children with cerebral palsy have non - progressive motor impairment that is often but not always associated with mental retardation. Lesions of the developing or immature brain cause their movement and postural disorders. In addition they often have other accompanying physical, behavioural, cognitive and communicative deficits. Briefly, cerebral palsy or CP is a non-progressive motor disorder resulting from brain injury prior to, during or after birth that results in a combination of developmental deficits.

Incidence

The incidence of cerebral palsy is said to be 2 to 2.5 per 1000 live births. Paradoxically, despite marked improvements in neonatal care, the incidence of CP seems to be increasing too. Though estimates vary, many children with CP may have some cognitive problems.

Characteristics

Cerebral palsy is characterised by an inability to fully control motor function. Depending on which part of the brain has been damaged and the degree of involvement of the central nervous system, one or more of the following may occur: spasms, tonal problems, involuntary movement, disturbance in gait and mobility, seizures, abnormal sensation and perception, impairment of sight, hearing or speech and mental retardation.

The most striking feature of children with cerebral palsy is the lack of muscular coordination and the concomitant physical disabilitics which affect their gait and movements. These physical characteristics often but not always, co exist with communication and cognitive difficulties. Children with CP may have difficulty with comprehension and expression of verbal and nonverbal communication. The extent of the communication disorder is generally linked to the severity of cerebral palsy as well as the presence and extent of mental retardation. The interplay of these two factors often determines the exact manifestation or the extent of the communication difficulties of a given child with cerebral palsy, in the continuum from a total lack of speech to almost negligible delay and deviations from normal speech.

A cerebral palsied child with severe motor impairment but minimal or no cognitive impairment will have receptive language on par with his normal peers but his speech will probably be well below that of his peers. On the other hand, another child with CP who has minimal motor impairment but is cognitively impaired to a greater extent, will have both his receptive and expressive language skills constrained by his overall cognitive abilities though his expressive speech may be far superior to that of the child without cognitive impairment. As a rule, the greater the motor impairment the greater the discrepancy between the receptive and expressive language skills of the child, and, the greater the cognitive impairment the greater the discrepancy between the chronological and language age of the child with the relative extent of the receptive and expressive language skills delay being determined by the additional impact of the motor disorder.

When a motor difficulty is present as it most often is, it affects all aspects of the child's speech production including the voice, articulation, speech initiation, sentence production, intonations, conversational and narrative abilities. It is estimated that over 70 per cent of CP children do have some problem with speech production. The speech of children with CP tends to be slow, jerky and irregular, laboured or effortful, and generally unintelligible. The lack of control over the respiratory patterns affects the voice resulting in breathiness, abrupt changes in pitch and volume and poor inflection. It also makes speech production slow and laboured with many unscheduled pauses. Given the effort involved in speech production, children with CP often limit their utterances to single words and short phrases.

Among the different subgroups of speech sounds, the child with CP produces the vowels and semivowels with relative ease. Productions of stop consonants like /m/ or /t/ which involve a single constriction in their production are relatively easy. On the other hand productions of consonants such as fricatives, trills and the sibilants, such as /f/, /r/ and /s/, which require fine coordination of the respiratory system and the articulators, are more difficult and highly variable both across individuals and within the same individual at different times. Consequently speech production patterns vary substantially across children with CP making it very difficult or almost impossible to draw a single or composite picture of the speech of children with cerebral palsy. The stages of language development, particularly expressive language, are also influenced by the difficulties in speech production and are affected in a similar manner.

Disorders

Movement disorders in children with cerebral palsy can be of different types and the subtypes of cerebral palsy are in fact identified on the basis of the type of movement disorder and the muscle tone. There are four main types of cerebral palsy: spastic, athetoid, ataxic, and mixed. Spastic cerebral palsy is an abnormality of muscle tone in which one or more extremities (arm or leg) are held in a rigid posture. Children with spastic CP have restricted movement. Children with ataxic cerebral palsy have difficulty making rapid or fine movements and walk unsteadily, with their legs widely spaced. The ataxic type of CP is characterised by low muscle tone and poor coordination of movements with an unsteady gait and tremors. These children are hypotonic or have poor muscle tone with an excessive range of movement and instability. Athetoid or dyskinetic cerebral palsy is a mixture of muscle tone which is hyper or hypotonic, that is too tight or loose. As a result children with dyskinetic CP have more complex movement disorders with involuntary movement and variable muscle tone, characterised by slow writhing movements, with poor motor initiation, direction and timing.

It is not always possible to strictly classify a child as having a particular subtype of CP. Mixed forms of cerebral palsy exist. It is common for patients to have more than one form of cerebral palsy. Consequent to these movement disorders children with CP may develop additional contractures and deformities over time. They are also at risk for joint dislocations. Cerebral palsy is usually accompanied by one or more associated problems including epileptic seizures, oral nutritional problems, visual problems, hearing deficits and at times mental retardation. Other disorders that are commonly seen associated with CP are respiratory illnesses, feeding and swallowing difficulties. When intervention for these difficulties is not provided, the child with CP can grow up having other psychological and behavioral problems with poor self-esteem.

Causes

Cerebral palsy does not have a single cause. It is a disorder caused by damage to the brain during pregnancy, delivery or shortly after birth. Risk factors linked with cerebral palsy include infection, seizure disorders, thyroid disorders, birth defects and Rh factor incompatibility. It is often the result of prenatal, perinatal or postnatal brain damage before the age of two years, including birth trauma, asphyxia, low birth weight and maternal disorders. Similar damage after the age of two years can be caused by acquired brain damage such as that consequent to meningitis or encephalitis. Though the characteristics of such acquired brain damage can be the same as CP it is seldom referred to by that term.

The damage to the brain results in a loss of appropriate muscular control and difficulty in the control of movements, including weak movements and poor coordination. A major symptom of cerebral palsy is the patient's difficulty to control and perform motor activities and poor motor coordination. These motor difficulties affect the overall development of the child right from breathing and feeding to the timely achicvement of developmental milestones such as the motor milestones as well as those of speech-language acquisition. Mastery of the physiological mechanisms that underlie the basic respiratory and vegetative activities such as breathing and feeding including sucking, swallowing, biting and chewing are often affected in the child with CP. It follows that the more complex non-vegetative movements that are based on these physiological systems, such as crying, laughing, coughing, phonation and articulation will also be affected. This lack of control over the basic vegetative and non-vegetative functions results in poor speech since the production of speech requires finely coordinated movements of these systems.

Assessment

Cerebral palsy is difficult to diagnose during early infancy. However, since early identification of cerebral palsy can lessen developmental problems and lead to appropriate intervention when it helps the most, it is important that the child who is suspected of having such a disorder requires a complete assessment by a neonatologist, to be followed by periodic checkups with his paediatrician and a developmental or paediatric neurologist. Evidence of other risk factors may aid the diagnosis. Children with cerebral palsy have varying degrees of physical disability and may also have associated medical problems which need to be assessed by a multidisciplinary team of specialists. Along with the paediatrician and neurologist, orthopaedic specialists are to be involved in the assessment of the movement disorder. Therapists and early interventionists such as occupational therapists and physiotherapists assess the feeding and locomotor difficulties of the child. SLPs and psychologists assess the communication and cognitive skills and needs of the child. Educators and special educators assess educational needs, including the educational placement needs of the child. A multidisciplinary team of specialists is therefore a must for the diagnosis and assessment of cerebral palsy.

Intervention

Given the range of difficulties that children with CP often face, they require the services of a wide range of specialists for comprehensive treatment and to help maximise and coordinate movement, as also minimise discomfort and pain. The clinical management of children with cerebral palsy involves both physicians and interventionists. The professionals that are involved in the management of the child with CP are the physician, physical and occupational therapists, social workers, speech-language pathologists, psychologists and educators.

Early intervention programmes are important in the management of children with CP. They are generally family-centred. Professionals and families work together with the child in specific activities. Medical management may include medication and orthodontic surgery or the use of orthotic aids such as splints. Physio and occupational therapists, speech- language pathologists, psychologists and educators can assist families by providing information and intervention. It is important for occupational therapy and physical therapy to begin soon after the diagnosis is made. Given the chewing, sucking and swallowing difficulties of the child with CP, the occupational therapist's guidance and training is often essential in establishing feeding patterns and ensuring adequate nutritional input to the child with CP. Similarly, without regular movement the muscles of the arms and legs can become weak and atrophied. Alternately they become rigidly fixed and form contractures. Special braces are often prescribed by the orthopaedic surgeon that helps prevent contractures by stretching spastic muscles. When combined with physiotherapy it can improve the child's motor development to a considerable extent.

As the child grows older the focus of therapy gradually shifts toward activities associated with daily living and communication. Exercises are designed to improve the child's ability to sit, move independently, and perform tasks such as dressing, writing, and toilet training. Orthotics can help control limb position, and walkers can help some children with CP, walk. Mastering such skills reduces demands on caregivers and helps the child obtain some degree of self-reliance, which helps build self-esteem.

Speech/language therapy helps the child overcome communication problems. Intervention for speech begins with helping the child to modify and adapt breathing patterns so as to ensure relaxed breathing patterns by reducing tension in the laryngeal and pharyngeal regions and stabilising the muscles of the trunk, neck and shoulder. Many children with cerebral palsy have problems speaking because of poor tone or uncontrolled movements in the muscles of the mouth and tongue. The speech therapist works along with the occupational therapist in stabilising the movements that are required for chewing, sucking and swallowing. Oromotor exercises and speech therapy help develop those muscles, improving both feeding and speech.

Articulation disorders are among the most common errors of speech that are seen in children with CP and are a direct concomitant of their motor difficulties. Articulation therapy such as those described in chapter 2 can help improve the quality of the speech of the CP child and make it more intelligible. However the overall results are constrained by the severity of the motor disorders.

Another aspect of speech-language therapy for the child with CP has to do with the particular combination of motor and cognitive deficits, if any, present in a particular child. A child with severe motor difficulties but with no cognitive deficit will have receptive language skills on par with his peers though his speech output and therefore his expressive language may lag far behind. It is important to acknowledge this capability of the child and not be misled by the poor speech output, in our dealings with such children. In contrast a child with minimal motor difficulties but with more severe cognitive deficits will have both his receptive and expressive language limited by his cognitive capabilities, though his speech per se may be fairly intelligible. When children with CP have additional complications or associated problems such as hearing loss, these will further complicate their speech-language development, necessitating additional intervention that addresses the needs of their limited hearing. Speech-language therapy for children with CP therefore has to address the particular profile of the given child and his particular needs. It could cover the entire range of therapeutic goals from stabilising basic oromotor movements and correcting articulation, to developing the different aspects of language including reading and writing.

Often the speech of the child with CP is more intelligible to the mother or the primary caregiver. At times this results in this individual interpreting the child's speech to other listeners. Well meaning as this is, it could have the undesirable effect of the child becoming too dependent on the caregiver as an interpreter. It is important that the child be given ample opportunity to express himself in a wide variety of settings, though this may be time consuming, as it has the more beneficial effect of building the child's confidence in his speech, which in turn will contribute towards its increasing intelligibility. Adequate speech stimulation and provision of opportunities to the child to express himself at his own pace are essential for the child to practice his speech and gain confidence in his ability to express himself. Parental goals for children with CP should be independence to the extent possible.

Alternate and Augmentative Communication (AAC)

Given the excellent language comprehension skills coupled with the constraints of the eventual speech output of some CP children with severe motor difficulties, there has been a move towards developing alternate and augmentative communication strategies for children with CP, particularly those among them with good receptive language skills but poor expressive language skills. These AAC techniques may cover a wide range of systems from the use of sign language to picture pointing and picture exchange, the usc of symbol systems such as the Blissymbols, and spelling through a letter board or computer screen with a range of pointing devices. Picture boards or other communication devices allow them to point to make their desires known. For school-age children or older persons with CP, there are a large number of augmentative communication devices, including shorthand typing programmes and computer-assisted speech devices. Children with CP who have good language capabilities but poor speech are able to benefit from communication technologies such as a computerised voice synthesizer.

It is important to know that the choice of an AAC depends on the age, capabilities and constraints of the child at a given time. As the condition changes and the child's capabilities increase, the AAC device may have to be upgraded. It is therefore best to be guided by the speech-language therapist who will evaluate the child's capabilities and needs while prescribing a particular type of AAC. It is also important to periodically evaluate the child's performance with the AAC device of the moment and introduce changes as and when needed.

Given the complex and varied nature of the difficulties of the child with CP, it is not surprising that the child with CP may have behavioral problems or emotional issues that affect psychological development and social interactions. These may require special intervention or treatment, including behavior modification programs or individual and family counseling. Further, additional deficits such as attention deficits and hyperactivity disorder can be present in children with CP, and may require appropriate behavioral, educational, and medical intervention.

School Support

Traditionally children with cerebral palsy have been educated in special schools or 'spastic societies' as they are referred to in India, since they may need the assistance of both interventionists and educators. The advantage of being in a special school for the CP child with severe motor difficulties is that the additional facilities and resources needed by the child are likely to be found at the centre and the child can receive education and therapy in the same location. Special schools are more likely to be equipped with the expertise and equipment that may not be available in a regular school. Special educators in special schools have both the training needed to successfully educate a child with special needs and the necessary specialised teaching equipment that can be essential in the academic success of children with CP.

With the recent shift towards mainstreaming and inclusive education of children with special needs, children diagnosed with CP who have average or above average intelligence are being integrated into regular schools with provisions made for their physical challenges. With the aid of assistive devices such as communication boards and speech synthesizers, they are capable of handling the school curriculum and achieving their full potential. Those who argue for mainstreaming the CP child into regular schools point out that being among children with many different kinds of disabilities in a single classroom in a special school, it is difficult to ensure that every child's unique educational needs, particularly of those who are relatively more capable, are being met. It is also argued that as a result of growing up in a segregated environment, children enrolled in special schools might find it difficult to function in the larger 'outside world' after they are done with their schooling having been in a special education facility until early adulthood. The behavioral problems seen in some children with CP are also ascribed to the environment of the special school and the consequent social isolation, by some. The latter argue that by mainstreaming children with CP, apart from the academic benefits, it provides the child with CP a more normal social environment in which to grow up. This has in fact been hailed as the most important benefit of inclusion. It has also been argued that an additional benefit would be the sensitisation of other 'typically' growing children to the potential and the needs of the child with a disability leading to a greater acceptance of disabilities as such and a reduction of the stigma attached to those with disabilities.

However it is generally conceded that special schools may be needed for the more severely involved children. It is important to remember that even severely affected children can benefit from education and training. The choice of school for the child with CP should be influenced by the presence and degree of mental impairment and physical impairment, as well as the facilities available in the area. Inclusion or mainstreaming the child in a regular school, may work well for the child with a relatively mild physical impairment and no particular need for specialised medical care. If the child has cognitive and communicative abilities that are age-appropriate, then he is involved in the regular curriculum, if necessary with some additional support necessitated by the physical needs. It is noteworthy that there have been instances of even severely handicapped children with CP participating and doing well in mainstream schools with the assistance of electrically powered wheelchairs, electronic speech output devices and computers. As in the general population there may be a few gifted students among those with CP. Gifted students who have cerebral palsy and have poor communication skills face many barriers because of their physical disabilities but there have been quite a few, including some in India, who have successfully overcome their disabilities to eventually lead fulfilling lives, and also contribute significantly both to the cause of others with CP and to their communities at large.

Mainstreaming and inclusion of the child with CP, has not happened much in India. Some of the difficulties in mainstreaming even cognitively capable children with CP lie in the necessity of physical modifications to be made in the school to create a barrier-free environment, as well as the lack of aides and special educators in regular schools. Considerations of the CP child should be taken into account in the construction of new schools and suitable environmental modifications must be made to existing schools wherever feasible. Laws that allow special provisions such as writers or the use of alternative modes of communication in school examinations were non-existent until the recent past. Even since they have come into existence, the authorities of regular schools seldom seem inclined to support the child with CP in availing of them. However some exceptional individuals with CP have crossed these barriers and have gone on to write about what it meant to them to grow up being different. The National Open School has provided alternate opportunities for the disabled child to catch up with his education at his own pace – this does not of course provide the social benefits of inclusion.

Parental Support

Much of the attention paid to the educational needs and overall care of children with cerebral palsy over the last two to three decades in India, has been largely due to the persistent efforts of dedicated parents who have set up 'spastic societies' in different regions of the country. Though their reach does not cover all of the needs of the cerebral palsied in the country, since many of them are based in the larger metropolitan cities, quite a few of them have successfully set up models worthy of emulation, in expanding their services widely through outreach programmes. With a growing emphasis on mainstreaming, even in India, families have to make an informed choice on mainstreaming their child by considering all of the factors involved. It is also important to periodically re-examine the issue in the light of the changing needs of the child and the facilities available, rather than treat the decision on mainstreaming or not, as a one time decision.

11

Autism Spectrum Disorders

Among the several developmental disorders of childhood, one that has gained the greatest prominence in the recent years and continues to hold centre stage is the group of childhood disorders known as Autism Spectrum Disorders (ASD) or autism. This disorder, once considered a rarity, has in the recent past shown a dramatic rise in prevalence. Given its complexities and debilitating nature, a lack of clear understanding of its cause and consequently thereof of the treatment, it has become the focus of much public debate and research.

Definition

The term 'autism' was first used by Leo Kanner in 1943, to describe children who were totally indifferent to other people and were very aloof. These children made little eye contact with other people, had severe language deficits and showed no desire to communicate with others, through speech or otherwise. Unlike their typically developing peers, these children also showed little interest in imaginative or pretend play and instead reacted to their environment in unusual ways. Ever since Kanner's description of these children, the term 'autism' has been used as a diagnostic label to refer to others who share similar characteristics. A second, more broader term—'pervasive developmental disorders' or PDD was introduced in 1980 to refer to others who shared some of the features of autism but not all of those listed by Kanner.

Over the years, the increasing identification of children with some but not all the features of autism has led to a broadening of the definition and criteria for diagnosis of autism to include the milder and more common forms. The phrase 'Autism Spectrum Disorders' is now increasingly used instead of 'autism' in recognition of the fact that a large range of qualitative abnormalities exists in this group of children. The term 'Autism Spectrum Disorders' includes 'autistic disorder' and the 'pervasive developmental disorders', which in turn includes subtypes that will be described below. A common characteristic shared by all these children is that they all have difficulty in acquiring language and in using it for social purposes.

There have been a few, controversial case reports of children with autism who are said to have 'recovered' from autism. As a rule, however, autism spectrum disorders (ASD) are seen as life-long disorders. While some individuals with autism have been documented to make enough progress to eventually lead productive, independent lives, most make substantial but restricted progress. Some remain very handicapped and show deterioration in adolescence.

Incidence and Prevalence

Older studies of autism estimated the prevalence of autism to be 4 to 5 in 10,000 children. At the turn of the current century the prevalence of ASD was estimated to be 1 in 1000. Some current studies estimate the prevalence of ASD to be more than 1 in 500 children with a few estimates going up to 1 in 160. Like most other developmental disorders, ASD is more common in boys than girls with a male: female ratio of 4:1. There is also a higher risk (50 per cent as compared with the normal population) of siblings of a child diagnosed with ASD, also being diagnosed with the same condition. Reliable estimations of prevalence of ASD are not available in India, but most clinicians attest to an increase in the number of children with ASD, in their clinical practice.

Characteristics

The characteristics of ASD are many and varied. However, there is no single developmental or behavioural deficit that can be named as being the characteristic of autism. Most children with ASD have deficits in the areas of communication, social interaction and behaviour.

One of the earliest signs of ASD is impairment in joint attention and pretend play. The term 'joint attention' refers to the ability of very young children to use eye contact and pointing, to share experiences with others. These behaviours are often used by infants below 18 months of age to obtain objects out of their reach or to simply draw the attention of the adult to the object. Children also bring objects that interest them to show them to adults. These behaviours that are referred to as joint attention are often lacking in children with ASD.

Lack of eye contact is one of the most notable features of ASD. Depending on the severity, children with ASD may make no eye contact and appear totally aloof. In milder forms of ASD, children may at times make eye contact or smile and hug, but these are either not consistent, not sustained, or may occur only when the child desires to do so and not as is the case with other typically growing children, in response to an adult's initiation. Lack of spontaneous social interaction and social/emotional reciprocity is considered a hallmark of ASD. Their inability to share interests and poor social responsiveness has a marked effect on peer relations in establishing which, they are particularly poor. They also exhibit lack of varied, imaginative and spontaneous play.

Children with ASD often have delays in language acquisition or develop unusual ways of communication. Many children with ASD are nonverbal and do not compensate for their lack of speech through nonverbal means such as gestures. Others who are verbal may seem like they have good language skills, but on closer examination it will be apparent that their language skills consist mostly of rote skills such as imitation of nursery rhymes or TV jingles and that they are unable to use language effectively for purposes of communication. Their utterances are often related to their own obsessive preoccupations and result in stereotyped, repetitive or idiosyncratic language. Children with ASD often parrot the speech produced by others in their environment, a phenomenon referred to as 'echolalia'. They fail to respond to the communication of others and seldom initiate or sustain a conversation. In addition they often have abnormalities of speech affecting such aspects as pitch, stress, rate, rhythm and intonation.

From a linguistic point of view the communication deficits of verbal children with ASD are characterised primarily as semantic-pragmatic deficits. The pragmatic deficits are, as described above, those that affect their conversational skills. At the semantic level, apart from showing delayed development and a restricted lexicon, they have a tendency to interpret words literally and as a result have enormous difficulty in interpreting social subtleties of language forms such as jokes, puns and sarcasm. Their syntax is essentially normal but may be limited in variety. Phonology is generally not affected in terms of producing the correct phonemes of language, but intonation is often limited and monotonous.

The intellectual functioning of children with ASD is also varied and can range from severe mental retardation to superior intellectual functioning. They are said to be better on rote and mechanical skills but poorer on higher order conceptual processes such as reasoning and abstraction. Many children with ASD also have good visual-spatial perceptual processes. Their performance skills, particularly when involving shapes, puzzles and mazes may be superior to their verbal skills. Others may have islands of abilities that match those of their normal peers, but not across all developmental areas. In addition, some children with ASD have some superior talents such as in art, music or mathematics. In the recent past the capacity to understand the mental states of others or 'mind reading' has been singled out, as a deficit that is particular to children with ASD and has been suggested to be the cause that underlies their social difficulties and awkwardness.

Finally, children with ASD are also characterised by unusual or odd stereotypic behaviour such as hand flapping, finger flicking or gazing, and obsession with particular objects/parts of objects or even compulsive sniffing. They may also be characterised by inflexible adherence to routines or rituals that serve no purpose and react with severe tantrums when disturbed, making their lives and that of their caretakers quite complicated. Like all other characteristics of ASD these too may range from being severe enough for the child to become socially isolated or so mild that the child can blend into social settings without his behaviour attracting the attention of others. These social/affective, communicative and cognitive/ behavioural characteristics are known as the triad of autistic symptoms and all children with ASD have one or more of these in varying degrees.

In addition to these three groups of characteristics, it is now being increasingly recognised and documented that children with ASD have additional sensorimotor characteristics, which are expressed in stereotypes such as hand flapping, or other sensitivities such as hyper and hypo functioning, across modalities such as touch, audition, vision and olfaction leading to unusual interests and obsessions. Specific difficulties in imitation and initiating motor executive functions are also being increasingly documented.

Disorders

The term Autism Spectrum Disorders is now used to refer to five subtypes of pervasive developmental disorders (PDD). In addition to autistic disorder, it includes pervasive developmental disorder-not otherwise specified (PDD-NOS), Asperger's syndrome, Rett syndrome, and childhood disintegrative disorder. As described above all children with autism exhibit some impairment in the three areas of social interaction, communication and behaviour.

A diagnosis of autism is made on the basis of the presence of the number of these characteristics across the three areas with onset before 3 years of age. The clinical patterns vary depending on severity. Some children may have acquired some of these skills and subsequently regressed after a period of relatively typical development, the regression typically setting in the second year.

When a child has some of the signs of autism but does not meet all the criteria for a diagnosis of autism then the more tentative diagnosis of PDD (NOS) is made. If additional features then appear to meet all the requirements for a diagnosis of autism, then the diagnosis can be changed from PDD-NOS to autism.

A third subtype of ASD known as Asperger's syndrome is characterised by some of the social deficits seen in autism, such as poor peer relationship, a lack of empathy and an obsessive focus on some topics. However these children are intelligent and do not have delays in language acquisition. Asperger's is therefore considered as representing a high-functioning form of autism. Children with Asperger's are not normally identified as early as the other subtypes. They are generally enrolled in schools and their abnormalities are not identified until school age. They attract attention by their eccentric behaviour (such as an obsessive preoccupation with the class attendance roll call) and their difficulty in interacting with peers. They may also have coordination difficulties. Regular classroom teachers are likely to see more of this particular subtype of ASD than the other subtypes.

A fourth subtype of ASD is Rett syndrome. Like many children with autism, those with Rett syndrome have a normal period of development in early infancy followed by a regression in hand skills during the first or second year of development. Their subsequent stereotypic hand movements such as hand wringing and deteriorating language, cognitive and social skills make them appear similar to autistic children. Unlike autism, however, the cause of Rett syndrome is identified as a specific genetic mutation and is more or less exclusively seen in girls.

The fifth type of PDD is called childhood disintegrative disorder. This is a relatively rare disorder whose onset is much later than the other PDDs and is characterised by profound deficits across all developmental areas.

Apart from these five subtypes of the autistic spectrum disorders there are also overlaps between mild forms of ASD and other developmental language disorders such as the SLI and SPD described in chapters 5 and 6.

Causes

Though Kanner's initial description of autism referred to a biological inability to make effective contact as the cause of autism, for several decades thereafter a widely held causative theory of autism ascribed the condition to psychological factors and to inadequate nurturance by cold uncaring, highly educated and sophisticated, 'refrigerated' mothers in particular. Since the 1980's and 1990's this unsubstantiated psychological theory has largely been discarded and most serious researchers in the area clearly go by the biological bases of ASD.

ASD is now generally believed to be a biologically based neurodevelopmental disability with a strong genetic basis (supported by twin studies). However no single cause of ASD has been identified as yet. Instead it is now seen as representing a heterogeneous neurogenetic disorder, i.e., it could be caused by a genetic vulnerability possibly triggered by other infectious and metabolic diseases such as congenital rubella, tuberous sclerosis, fragile X syndrome and untreated phenylketonuria. Another hypothesis that is widely held is that the measles-mumps-rubella (MMR) vaccine was associated with an increased risk of ASD. Since children with ASD often also suffer from seizures, a neurological basis is postulated. Since the 1990s, an increasing number of neuroimaging and autopsy studies have shown developmental brain abnormalities suggesting that ASD can be caused by neurological insult in the early prenatal period.

Apart from these neuroanatomical abnormalities, quantitative neurochemical abnormalities have also been found in serotonin, dopamine and opioids. However it must be remembered that as of date there is no laboratory test that is specific to ASD and it continues to be defined by the presence or absence of the constellation of characteristics described above which are probably the result of multiple causes including genetic, neuropathologic and environmental.

Referral and Assessment

Identification of children with ASD is most often carried out by a systematic enquiry about aspects of development of the given child in all of the areas described above, supplemented by observations of the child's behaviour. Whenever there is a suspicion of the child's development in these areas not being appropriate to his age and if there appears to be a cluster of these developmental abnormalities across the areas described above, the child should be referred to a multidisciplinary team that has expertise in this area, for a formal evaluation. A discussion with the child's parents regarding any concerns they might have about their child's social or language skills, coupled with observations of the child will help clarify whether a referral is warranted. Early diagnosis is important for more than one reason. Given the possibility of an underlying genetic cause, the parents of the child should have this information early, so as to enable them to take informed decisions regarding additions to the family. It is also crucial for long term results, in view of the fact that it is now clear that the earlier the intervention the better the long term outcome.

An assessment for a child with suspected PDD involves seeking and ruling out other conditions that may account for the child's behaviour and then assessing the given child on evaluation tools that are specific to ASD to arrive at a definitive diagnosis. The criteria specified in the Diagnostic and Statistical Manual (DSM-IV) are widely used by physicians. There are also several standardised tools such as the Childhood Autism Rating Scale (CARS), the Autism Diagnostic Interview-Revised (ADI-R) and the Autism Diagnostic Observation Schedule (ADOS), that have been developed in the West and are being used in India. These are further supplemented by specific assessment tools for the assessment of social behaviour or communication and language skills.

Intervention

Despite the concerted efforts of many organisations around the world, there is as yet no medical cure available for children with ASD. This state of affairs is to be seen in the context of the lack of understanding about the cause of autism. There is, however, a plethora of intervention strategies that is advocated and used but no consensus regarding the best intervention strategy.

The management of autism has undergone radical changes since it was first identified. In the 1950s when the etiological theories were parent-centred, management focused on psychotherapy with parents. With the etiological theories changing to emphasis of theories of organic origin or the biological basis of autism, management procedures too have moved away from these early psychotherapeutic models. While some biological interventions are being tried out, the most widespread intervention strategies are developmental, behavioural and educational. There is now evidence that intensive early intervention can have a significant positive impact on long-term prognosis. Several intervention approaches have been developed but there is no consensus on which is the most effective. Strategies that are tailored for the needs of the individual child and family and aim at improving the overall functional skills of the child in the areas of concern, that is, social interaction, communication and behaviour are found to be the best. For the best results these programmes have to be started early and used consistently. In Western countries like the USA and UK, the laws of the country have mandated early intervention for these children below the age of 3 years, with a subsequent shift to local schools after the age of 3 years along with therapeutic and family support.

There is as yet no medical or pharmacological cure for autism. However some ASD interventionists from a medical background have advocated management procedures which include providing the child with nutritional supplements such as large doses of Vitamin E, or putting the children on a diet which eliminates milk and wheat products. Still others have advocated measures such as chelation therapy, which is based on a hypothesis that autism is caused by toxins in the child's body that need to be eliminated. None of these methods have however been unequivocally proven but all of them have their share of staunch supporters and detractors. In addition, physicians are often involved in health care measures that relate to some of the causative factors such as fragile X syndrome or tuberous sclerosis and in the management of co-morbid conditions such as convulsions.

Physicians are also involved in the management of hyperactivity, sleep disorders, stereotypy and harmful behaviour such as aggression and self injurious behaviour, which might involve medication. It is best to target the most disruptive of these behaviours first to facilitate positive behaviours such as communication, socialisation and learning. These behaviours also change from time to time with newer ones appearing with elimination of existing behaviours. Children with ASD also are at a higher risk of psychopathologic problems such as mood disorder, anxiety disorders, attention-deficit/hyperactivity disorder, and obsessive-compulsive disorder. The prescription and monitoring of medication should be done by referral to a developmental paediatrician, child neurologist, or child psychiatrist.

The most popular intervention programmes, until recently, for children with autism have been those based on behaviour modification principles and theories such as 'Applied Behaviour Analysis (ABA) and 'Verbal Behaviour Analysis' (VBA). The approach emphasises the behavioural approach for training the children in compliance, imitation, and language acquisition in repeated discrete behavioural trials. The entire management is done in a meticulously controlled and documented fashion and has produced measurable results. Consequently the approach has become increasingly popular and several models within the applied behavioural approach (such as the VBA) have been developed and used widely.

Another widely used and increasingly popular approach to the management of autism is the Sensory Integration Approach (SIT) advocated and practised by occupational therapists. This approach is based on the hypothesis that many of the difficulties that are faced by the child with ASD are caused by their sensory processing difficulties and emphasis is therefore placed on helping the child cope with these difficulties through sensory integration techniques. Occupational and physical therapy are also helpful in children with coordination and motor planning deficits.

Several intervention approaches for children with ASD acknowledge the communication deficits of these children as a core deficit and have addressed the communication difficulties per se. There is however wide variation between the rationale of these approaches and their content. Thus for instance while intervention methods such as 'Auditory Integration Training' (AIT) aim at 'rectifying' the child's auditory hypersensitivity through exposure to filtered or modified auditory stimuli through mechanical means, visual interventions such as Picture Exchange Communication System (PECS) aims at circumventing the child's difficulty with aural-oral speech by enabling him to communicate through an alternate mode such as exchanging pictures. Facilitated communication (FC) on the other hand is a technique in which a trained facilitator enables a nonverbal child to communicate through writing, typing or pointing to letters on a letter board by supporting the person's arm or hand physically, while the child uses a typewriter, computer keyboard, or communication device.

In the recent past, speech-language therapy is recognised as having an important role in the management of children with ASD. The communication deficits seen earlier as a symptom of autism are now being acknowledged as being at the core of autism and techniques to improve speech-language skills are found to be valuable in bettering the overall condition of the child with ASD. Speech-language assessments and intervention cover many aspects of communication such as semantics and pragmatics as also voice and articulation. Behavioural techniques are also employed by SLPs to enhance language skills. Children who receive speech-language therapy early on have been reported to retain these skills contributing to their overall long-term prognosis.

In addition to these more widely advocated and well-grounded therapies, there are a host of other specific approaches to the management of children with ASD such as Teaching and Educating Autistic Children and Children with other Communication Handicaps (TEACCH), Floor Time and Relationship Development Intervention (RDI). The former, that is TEACCH, focuses on the individual with autism and provides a broad based intervention strategy that builds on the existing skills and interests of that individual. The latter is based on offering intensive relationship based interventions that are within the developmental framework as opposed to the more rigid behavioural interventions.

Apart from these better established and better known intervention approaches, there are several alternative therapies such as homeopathy and Reiki which are advocated and used fairly widely. Many of these therapies, including some described above are anecdotal in nature and are propagated as being harmless while possibly resulting in remarkable/ miraculous changes. They have seldom been investigated in carefully designed, controlled studies to support their claims.

The general trend currently, however, is to provide intervention that is early and intensive within a behavioural or developmental framework. These include components of behaviour training, speech-language therapy including augmentative communication methods, occupational therapy and development of social interactions. Parent training is often included. Medical management is suggested when necessary and parents often pursue alternative therapies. It is not uncommon to find several strategies being used for the same child at any given time.

There is now increasing consensus that what works best for children with ASD in the long run, are programmes that provide intensive early intervention, which provide individualised services for children and families. These programmes need to have multidisciplinary input with a curriculum that emphasises a supportive environment but use systematic and structured teaching that include imitation, language, play and social interaction. A predictable routine is emphasised with behavioural problems being addressed within a functional approach and the transition to regular school being planned to enable a smooth transition and eventual integration. The outcome of these services is better when provided before the age of 5 years – the earlier the better in fact, resulting in better educational progress, higher measured IQ and better adaptive behaviour. As reported by the U.S. National Research Council in 2001, "intensive early intervention for children with ASD makes a clinically significant difference for many children—better than expected gains in IQ scores, language, autistic symptoms, future school placements and several measures of social behaviour". When provided with adequate early support several children with ASD and nearly all with Asperger's can successfully go through school and college education in the mainstream. While they may continue to have social and behavioural oddities, they are able to function within the society along with family and friends.

As elsewhere, the incidence and prevalence of ASD is also found to be increasing in India, in recent years. However, facilities such as diagnostic and intervention services have not kept pace. Apart from some basic services being provided by national institutions such as NIMHANS, Bangalore and NIMH, Secunderabad, there is hardly any focused and sustained effort on the part of the government agencies. Several NGOs, frequently involving affected parents, on the other hand, have established parent forums and special centres/schools (such as Action for Autism and Tamanna in New Delhi, Forum for Autism, Mumbai and ASHA in Bangalore) that cater to the needs of children with ASD.

In view of the near total lack of facilities for early intervention for children with ASD and other communication disorders (described in the earlier chapters), in India, and the ever increasing demand for quality services, this author initiated a programme called the Communication DEALL program in the year 2000. Communication DEALL (Developmental Eclectic Approach to Language Learning) is an early intervention program for children with communication disorders such as SLI, PLI, DVD, PDD and Autism, whose aim is successful integration of these children in regular schools, with intensive preschool intervention. It is our belief that successful mainstreaming of children with developmental disabilities can only be achieved with adequate preparation in the preschool years. Intervention for developmental disabilities is, more often than not, long-term in nature and has to be provided on a sustained basis over a prolonged period of time. The high therapist to client ratio required for such preparation and the consequent costs are major constraints. However, we are convinced that the long-term economics of an integrated independent child as against a dependent child in a special programme, justifies this initial cost. Another major drawback is the delay in identification and referral. Ideally, enrolment in DEALL should take place by the age of 2 ½ years – 3 ½ years, before the condition has become far too complex to be handled in an early intervention programme; giving the child the maximum possibility of attaining age appropriate skills by the school entry age of 5 ½ years. It is our intention to establish the Communication DEALL programme as a viable model, that with training can be replicated as and where needed, in order to serve the requirements of an ever-increasing number of children with developmental language disorders including those with the Autism Spectrum Disorders; within their community. We are now being supported in this endeavour by the Navajbai Ratan Tata Trust, Mumbai.

School Support

Given that many children with ASD have adequate intellectual skills, many of them can function well in regular schools. It is important however that the school provide a supportive environment that is both understanding and encouraging. Children with ASD in regular classroom are some times misclassified as having learning disabilities. Children in the ASD spectrum including those with Asperger's often have special educational needs. However they benefit to a great extent by being with typically developing peers who often incidentally serve as models for appropriate behaviour.

Their social and language skills in particular benefit from inclusion in a regular school environment. It is however important that the classroom placement is based on the developmental skills and behavioural issues involved, to suit the child's best interest. The resources available to the school and family, are also a consideration.

Not much research has been done on the effectiveness of various curricula and programs for children with ASD. It is however recognised that the teaching environment should be highly supportive of the child's learning needs and involve the systematic teaching of skills. A programme that is predictable and routine, which provides structure, direction, and organisation for the child and takes into account his or her overall developmental status and specific strengths and deficits, is ideal. Programmes such as TEACCH include comprehensive educational curricula that have been developed specifically for children with ASD. They emphasise the importance of observing each individual child and improving the adaptation of that child through new skills and environmental changes rather than being influenced by theories on autism. Comprehensive assessments and structured teaching are considered important for skill enhancement. Emphasis is also placed on an acceptance of an individual child's deficits and providing a holistic treatment.

The communication environment at school is crucial and should providc adcquate opportunities for the child with ASD to have successful communication and social interaction. Children with ASD find the directive styles easier but need to acquire the communicative skills required to deal with nondirective styles. The class teacher can play a facilitatory role in environmental arrangement to increase initiation of communication and support to promote active and independent participation in activities. The management of behavioural problems can also be integrated with communication strategies. The child needs to be trained to use communication to mutually regulate behaviour in peer interaction by acquiring socially acceptable means to protest and reject.

In addition they need to be trained in independent strategies to deal with anxiety arousing situations through relaxation and other calming activities or through requests for opting out of these situations. For the child who is nonverbal and is using assistive or alternative communication modes, the teacher needs to be familiar with the mode of communication.

These may include manual sign systems (ASL, Tokens), visual graphic symbols (PECS), facilitated communication for hyperlexics and voice-output communication aids. It should also be remembered that the selection of an assistive or alternate communication system is not a one time process but changes according to the needs and capabilities of the child. At times more than one system may be used with the emphasis being on flexibility and the creative use of language across a variety of situations.

Behavioural strategies to increase compliance and decrease undesirable behaviour should also be used in the classroom. These management protocols should be the same at school and home. Typically developing children in the classroom often serve as role models for those with ASD. Positive reinforcements are more conducive to overall development than punishment, which should be limited to specific situations. Being trained in these behaviour management procedures can be helpful to both teachers and parents.

Teaching social skills is another important aspect of the training of the child with ASD, as even when they acquire the more basic skills, they still need help in promoting their social competence. In clinics and regular classrooms, social stories are increasingly used to facilitate appropriate social behaviour in children with ASD and generalise these skills to social settings.

Parental Support

Parental support is an indispensable aspect of the management of children with ASD. The process begins with conveying the diagnosis to parents. Nearly all parents go through a prolonged period of intense agony when their child receives a diagnosis of ASD and need all the support they can get. Genetic counselling and behavioural observations of any other siblings are also a must given that there is a higher incidence of autism in siblings of children diagnosed with ASD. Behavioural skills training provide the parent and other family members with the much needed skills to manage and support their child's development, at home. Most intervention programmes have specific components that address parental issues that aim at reducing the stress that parents face. Parent education and empowerment is also essential in obtaining the much needed advocacy for the understanding, acceptance and rights of children with ASD

Our understanding of the spectrum, etiology, diagnosis, and management of ASD in children has changed dramatically over the past two decades. Recently developed screening and diagnostic tools have made early identification and referral to developmental and educational programmes possible. Thus, there is a growing body of evidence that early and appropriate intervention may indeed have a positive impact on overall outcome - the disabling aspects of ASD can be minimised to such a degree that, although not cured, more children with autism will indeed be able to live independently as adults.

12
Other Neuropsychiatric Disorders

In addition to the major subtypes of developmental language disorders described in this section, there are several neuropsychiatric disorders in children, which include communication deficits among their major symptoms. Some of these disorders will be described briefly here.

Traumatic Brain Injury (TBI)

Among the most common causes of speech-language deficits that are seen in school children is TBI or traumatic brain injury. TBI refers to an external injury of sufficient force to affect the normal functioning of the brain. These injuries may be the result of child abuse such as the 'shaken baby syndrome' or by falls, accidents and assaults. The consequences of these injuries are dependent on their severity and the age of the child at the time of the injury and can range from mild word finding difficulties or unclear speech to life-long impairments in motor, language and cognitive functions. When a typically developing child in preschool or school suffers from injuries to the brain, it halts, impedes and interferes with the reacquisition of a wide range of interdependent sensory, motor, behavioural and language abilities.

The speech-language deficits that are commonly observed in children who suffer TBI are both receptive and expressive. They include difficulties in auditory comprehension of verbal and nonverbal stimuli despite normal hearing, including difficulty in pointing to common objects that are named and in following simple verbal instructions. They can also have expressive language difficulties such as naming common objects, repeating words and sentences and describing things and events. Some may retain their earlier expressive language skills but lose the clarity of speech and their verbal fluency, i.e. become dysarthric. In extreme cases the child may become totally mute. Reading and writing skills if acquired prior to the injury may also be affected with decreased reading comprehension and difficulty in writing. In addition children with TBI often suffer from attention and memory deficits. They are unable to sustain attention in class and recall recent events including what was taught in the previous lessons. All of these deficits will in turn affect their learning and participation in school activities. Depending on the level of functioning and recovery, the child with TBI too has to be placed back in the mainstream with adequate support for his post traumatic difficulties. Like other children with developmental communication disorders he too will need specialised services and additional support from his class teacher for reintegration in school. The clinicians will work at improving and teaching compensatory skills necessary for communication along with individually planned treatment procedures that focus on areas of cognitive processing abilities, attention, memory, problem solving and organisational strategies for recovery of language skills. This is best achieved in collaboration with doctors and other related professionals along with teachers and parents within the multidisciplinary approach. The course of recovery will range from provision of all of the supportive therapies over a prolonged period of time until such time that he is ready to be brought back to school with gradual fading of supportive therapies and increased support from the classroom teacher. Even a child who has apparently 'recovered fully' is likely to have difficulty in sustaining attention in class, subtle difficulties in processing language in real time and retaining it in his memory, and these subtle difficulties have to be considered by the teacher in classroom management. At times personality changes such as a short temper and aggressiveness may also be seen in children who were gentle and well mannered prior to the injury. These changes in the child should be recognised as being caused by the head injury and treated accordingly.

Attention Deficit Hyperactivity Disorder (ADHD)

There is now an increasing awareness of the possibility of a close relationship between communication and psychiatric disorders. It has been documented that there is a high incidence of communication or language disorders in children diagnosed with mental or psychiatric disorders in childhood such as ADHD, oppositional and or conduct disorders, disruptive behaviour disorders and emotional disorders. The communication disorders seen in these children range from isolated speech disorders including the dysarthrias and apraxias to delayed language acquisition, difficulty in abstract language, semantic-pragmatic deficits and poor social communication. The hypotheses in terms of the cause and effect relationship between the communication disorders and psychiatric disorders vary. While some researchers and clinicians see them both as being caused by the same biological cause, others speculate that early communication difficulties could lead to secondary psychiatric problems. A third group of scientists postulates a developmental interaction between the two, each exacerbating the other. Isolated speech disorders are less likely to be seen along with psychiatric disorders, whereas language disorders are seen to coexist or co-occur with psychiatric disorders more frequently. This could be attributed to the spiralling effect of a language disorder, particularly when unidentified and inadequately supported. Often psychiatric disorders are seen to emerge in healthy children with undetected language disorders. This is particularly true of children with subtle auditory processing deficits.

The root cause of ADHD, like in so many other developmental disabilities is not known for sure as yet. However, it is generally considered to be due to neurological causes which might be genetic in disposition. Other factors such as parental smoking and alcohol consumption (during pregnancy) are considered exacerbating factors. The evaluations for a child suspected of having ADHD include medical evaluations to rule out other medical causes, psychological, audiological and speech-language evaluations.

The communication skills of children with ADHD have not been given much importance until recently. This was largely due to the fact that while in a small proportion of children with ADHD there may be a co-morbid speech-language delay, a majority of them do not show a lag in initial language development. However, it has become increasingly clear that there is a strong association between language deficits and behaviour problems in children. Research in this area has revealed that poor expressive and/or receptive language skills are more common in children with antisocial behaviour problems.

As discussed in the earlier chapters, language competence is critically important for successful social and academic functioning. Until recently there has not been much of a focus on the communication skills of children diagnosed with ADHD since most of them do not exhibit early developmental lags in language acquisition. However, given the persisting academic difficulties of these children and an increased awareness of the role of higher language skills in academic success some investigations have begun to focus on the linguistic skills of children with ADHD. There is now some evidence emerging that listening comprehension and working memory are impaired in children with ADHD, irrespective of their language development. Listening skill and working memory are, however, crucial for higher level language development and are likely to be related to the increasing difficulty of children with ADHD in higher grades.

Audiological assessments for children with ADHD are suggestive of central auditory processing difficulties in them. These children even when they do not have frank language impairment, perform poorly as compared to their peers on listening comprehension tasks. While their performance on straight-forward factual questions was comparable to other children their age and better than those of their peers with language impairment, on tasks that needed inference on the basis of verbal material presented to them, they performed poorly in comparison with their typically growing peers. They were also poor at detecting errors in information presented to them. Interestingly these subtle language processing difficulties of these children correlated with the degree of ADHD. This correlation was particularly strong with ratings of attention difficulty and is the most likely reason underlying the academic difficulties of these children.

When the child with ADHD is having problems following the complex information that is provided verbally in the classroom, because of his comprehension difficulties, he is likely to show poor compliance and an inability to complete tasks. These listening comprehension difficulties may indeed underlie both his academic and behavioural problems. As the child moves into higher grades this may be particularly so, since the demands on accurate and efficient comprehension of new information, provided largely through verbal means, increases in the higher grades. These comprehension difficulties could also affect peer interaction and social relations which depend considerably on accurate comprehension of complex verbal information. Thus it is likely that some of the core behaviours of ADHD could be linked to, or be a consequence of the comprehension difficulties of the child.

Given the difficulties of the child with ADHD in auditory verbal comprehension, it is essential that assessments of language skills and functioning are carried out routinely for them. It is quite likely that children with ADHD could have co-occurring but undetected language problems. In addition to poor social communication and consequent poor social skills, these language deficits may even lead to a lack of inner speech and consequent behavioural disinhibition. Therefore, intervention measures that do not take these into account will have only limited success. The schoolteacher needs to be sensitive to the oral and written language skills of the child with ADHD though superficially it might appear that the child has adequate language skills.

Intervention for children with ADHD can also be varied. Pharmacological intervention often involves the prescription of stimulants. However, because of the side effects of these medications, they have to be considered carefully. Behavioural and behavioural-cognitive approaches are also used for children with ADHD. With the increasing sensitivity to communication difficulties of children with ADHD, communication intervention focusing on listening environment modification and listening skills enhancement along with a more scheduled and structured communicative environment is advocated.

As in all developmental disabilities parents play a crucial role in helping children with ADHD to achieve a positive developmental and educational experience. Parents often need to be guided by the teacher to become aware of the possibility of a disorder that underlies the child's academic difficulties, the course of action to be taken in terms of consultations and assessments, as well as long-term management and outcomes. The teacher's involvement and observation in monitoring medication and its effect during school time will help the physician and the family in arriving at an appropriate dosage and schedule for a given child so at to maximise its benefits and reduce the impact of side effects. In class, the teacher can place him near the front of the class and provide cues to remind him to stay on task. It is also important to monitor and coordinate school and home progress through frequent telephone or one on one contact with the parents.

Both the parent and the teacher of a child with ADHD should work out a system of holding the child accountable for his work. These parents will also require additional help with monitoring and completing homework. For instance, children with ADHD may not be able to attend to their work if the television is on. It would help to fix a specific time for the child to complete his homework and switch the television off during that time. Children with ADHD are also likely to do better in short and perhaps more frequent sessions of homework than being asked to do all of it at one go. Computer based programs that provide immediate feedback on accuracy can be beneficial. Equally important is adult supervision with set ground rules.

Another important skill that is specifically to be monitored for ADHD children at school are their peer relations. Children with

ADHD show a wide range of deficits in social behaviour. While some of them are gregarious and popular with their peers, others can have significant social difficulties and withdrawal. While the former are often impulsive and have to be curbed in this respect, the latter have to be facilitated by encouraging social interaction.

As the child with ADHD grows into adolescence, it is important for both the parent and the teacher to step down the direct monitoring and supervision of his work and encourage him to take greater responsibility for his own work. It may be useful to take the child into confidence and educate him about his condition so that he may have adequate knowledge of his strengths and weaknesses, in order to make the best of them. If handled properly, this can instil in the child positive self-esteem and self-confidence.

This would be a first step towards enabling the child to develop an attitude of responsibility for his actions.

Other Childhood Syndromes

In addition to TBI and ADHD, there are a number of other childhood neuropsychiatric syndromes in which one sees speech-language disorders. Since they are rare and do not occur in very large numbers, a few of the more common types are briefly described below.

Landau Kleffner Syndrome (LKS)

LKS is an acquired language disorder that occurs in a child who has already acquired language. It is also described as an acquired aphasia with convulsive disorder since it is often but not always accompanied by convulsions. It occurs most often in children between the ages of 5–9 years. At times it is preceded by a viral infection, epilepsy or minor head trauma. As a consequence, the child's receptive language skills deteriorate first, followed by deterioration in expressive language. This deterioration can be acute, that is sudden or prolonged over a period of time.

LKS is a disorder whose underlying cause is as yet not clearly known. Prognosis and treatment are consequently uncertain. The outcome is varied across children. Some children experience rapid losses followed by rapid gains. Others progressively deteriorate with or without convulsions. It is generally believed that the older the child is at onset of the disorder, the better the prognosis. All efforts should be made to reintegrate the child with LKS into the regular classroom, but this would of course be subject to the extent of deterioration and recovery. Since they experience particular difficulty in the auditory mode, the visual mode may be given preference in educating them.

Fragile X

This is a genetic developmental disorder caused by a mutation on the X-chromosome that is largely seen in boys but could also be present in girls. These children are characterised by learning difficulties and mental retardation and often exhibit signs of autism. Many of them have a language deficit, which affects expressive language in particular. Their speech is often jocular and repetitive in nature. With the element of retardation present the long term outcome has to be planned keeping this in mind. Given the genetic nature of the disorder, parental awareness is crucial.

There are several other congenital childhood syndromes with genetic anomalies, such as Cretinism, Cri du chat syndrome, Klinefelter's syndrome, Mobius syndrome, Prader Willis syndrome and Turner's syndrome in which the speech-language development will be affected in addition to other developmental abnormalities. These conditions though are relatively rare and are likely to be recognised and attended to by the parent, given the abnormalities in overall development. In other congenital syndromes such as Pierre Robin Syndrome and Treacher Collins syndrome, specific abnormalities of the facial region including cleft palates will be present with concomitant speech disorders.

In yet other syndromes such as Gilles de la Tourette syndrome, symptoms such as facial tics and changes in communication, such as the excessive use of violent and obscene language may appear during late childhood, that is, before twelve years and should be referred to the physician.

In addition to the above, infections such as rubella, cytomegalovirus and herpes simplex may also affect communication skills in children. Conditions such as substance or excessive alcohol abuse by pregnant mothers can lead to conditions such as foetal alcohol syndrome or HIV in the parent leading to childhood HIV that can result in a communication disorder in the child, either by itself or in combination with other developmental disorders and it would be advisable for the teacher to be aware of the same.

Appendices

Appendix A—Further Reading

Ahluwalia, H.P.S & J.P. Singh. 2006. *International Conference on Human Resource Development in the Area of Disability Rehabilitation*, New Delhi: Kanishka Publishers.

Ahluwalia, H.P.S & J.P. Singh. 2004. *Summit of the Mind*, New Delhi: Kanishka Publishers.

Ahluwalia, H.P.S. 2003. *Disability Status India*, New Delhi: Rehabilitation Council of India.

Banerjee, Gautam. 2004. *Legal Rights of Persons With Disability*, New Delhi: Rehabilitation Council of India.

Bantawal, Anuradha. 2006. *Fundamentals of Hearing, Hearing Impairment and Audiological Management*, DSE (HI) Manual, New Delhi: Rehabilitation Council of India and Kanishka Publishers.

Greene M.C.L & L. Mathieson. 1995. *The Voice and its Disorders*, London: Whurr Publishers.

Immanuel, Prabakar, Claudia Koenig and Sian Tesni. 1988. *Listening To Sounds and Signs: Trends in Education and Communication*, Bangalore: Christoffel-Blindenmission and Books For Change.

Jalvi, Rajeev. 2006. *Introduction to Hearing Impairment*, DSE (HI) Manual, New Delhi: Rehabilitation Council of India and Kanishka Publishers.

Jha, Madan M., Priti Joshi, Renu Singh and Subir Shukla. 2005. *Towards Inclusive Education*, New Delhi: Rehabilitation Council of India.

Karanth, Prathibha and Joe Rozario (ed.). 2003. *Learning Disabilities in India*, New Delhi: Sage Publications.

Kundu, C.L. 2000. *Status of Disability in India*, New Delhi: Rehabilitation Council of India.

Lees, Janet and Shelagh Urwin. 1995. *Children with Language Disorders*, New Delhi: Laxman Chand Arya.

Mary Sr., Rita. *Manual on Maternal Reflective Method*, New Delhi: Rehabilitation Council of India.

Morris, David W.H. 1993. *Dictionary of Communication Disorders*, New Delhi: A.I.T.B.S. Publishers & Distributors.

Narayanaswamy, Saraswathy. 2006. *Family Community and the Hearing Impaired Child*, DSE (HI) Manual, New Delhi: Rehabilitation Council of India and Kanishka Publishers.

Patel, Purushottam G. 2004. *Reading Acquisition in India*, New Delhi: Sage Publications.

Prasad, Janardan. 2006. *Education of the Handicapped Children: Problems and Solutions*, New Delhi: Kanishka Publishers.

Position Paper. 2006. *National Focus Group on Education of Children with Special Needs*, New Delhi: NCERT.

Puri, M. and G. Abraham. 2004. *Handbook of Inclusive Education for Educators, Administrators and Planners: Within Walls, Without Boundaries*, New Delhi: Sage Publications.

RCI. *Training Manual on Disability Management and Mainstreaming of Persons with Disability for University and Management Institutions*, New Delhi: Rehabilitation Council of India.

Reddy, G. L., R. Ramar and A. Kusuma. 2004. *Hearing Impairment: An Educational Consideration*, Special Education Series, New Delhi: Discovery Publishing House.

Shukla, Indira. 2006. *Education of Children with Hearing Impairment*, DSE (HI) Manual, New Delhi: Rehabilitation Council of India and Kanishka Publishers.

Singh, Bharat. 2006. *Modern Special Education*, New Delhi: Anmol Publications.

Singh, A.N. 2005. *Enabling the Differently Able: Concepts, Education and Community*, New Delhi: Shipra Publications.

Tahiliani, H. 2004. *Learning Disability: A Remedial Reading Programme*, Delhi: Gagan Deep Publications.

Tharyani, D.K. 2006. *Curricular Strategies and Adaptations for Children with Hearing Impairment*, DSE (HI) Manual, New Delhi: Rehabilitation Council of India and Kanishka Publishers.

Venkatesh, S. 2004. *Children with Developmental Disabilities*, New Delhi: Sage Publications.

Warrick, A. and S. Kaul. 1997. *Their Manner of Speaking, Augmentative Communication for Children and Young Adults with Severe Speech Disorders*, Calcutta: Indian Institute of Cerebral Palsy.

Appendix B—Some Relevant Websites

http://www.aiishmysore.com
http://www.ayjnihh.nic.in
http://www.communicationdeall.org
http://www.drmvst.ac.in
http://www.speechear.org
http://www.iccons.org
http://www.rehabcouncil.nic.in
http://www.asha.org
http://www.slpsite.com
http://www.hyperlexia.org/sp1.html
http://www.eduref.org
http://www.eric.ed.gov/searchdb/index.html

Appendix C—Referral Sources

Some organisations that offer services for the communication disordered in India.

All India Institute of Speech & Hearing, Manasagangothri, Mysore 570 006.

Ayjnihh Bandra Reclamation, Bandra (W), K.C. Marg, Mumbai 400 050.

Com Deall, No. 47, Hutchins Road 2nd Cross, Cookes Town Bangalore 560 084.

Deptt. of Ent Pgimer, Chandigarh 160 012.

Deptt. of ENT, CMC Hospital, Vellore 632 004.

Deptt. of ENT, CMC Hospital, Coimbatore 641 018.

Deptt. of ENT, JIPMER Hospital, Pondicherry 605 006.

Deptt. of Speech & Hearing, Manipal College of Allied Health Sciences, Manipal 576104.

ICCONS, J.M Institute of Speech and Hearing, Road No. 5, Indrapuri Patna 800 024.

M.V. Shetty College of Speech and Hearing, A.B. Shetty Circle, Mangalore 575 001.

National Trust, 4 Vishnu Digamber Marg, New Delhi 110 002.

National Institute of Mental Health and Neuro Sciences, Wilson Gardens, Bangalore 560 029.

National Institute of Mental Health, P.O. Bowen Pally, Secundrabad 500 011.

Rehabilitation Council of India, B-22, Qutub Institutional Area, New Delhi 110 016.

Regional Rehabilitation & Training Centre, Bairoi, Cuttack 754 010.

Regional Rehabilitation Centre, B.T. Road, Bonhooghly, Calcutta 700 090.

RUAS, Deptt. of ENT, All India Institute of Medical Sciences, Ansari Nagar, New Delhi 110 029.

S.R. Chandrashekar Institute of Speech and Hearing, Hennur Road, Bangalore 560 084.

School of Audiology and Speech Therapy, B.Y.L. Nair Hospital, Mumbai 400 008.

Index